Train Up a Child

Darnell Zollinger Jeffs

Deseret Book Company
Salt Lake City, Utah

To my mother and father

©Deseret Book Company
All rights reserved
Printed in the United States of America
First printing April 1983
Library of Congress Catalog Card No. 83-070706
ISBN 0-87747-963-1

Contents

Chapter 1

Establish a Loving Relationship

Train up a child in the way he should go:
and when he is old, he will not depart from it.
(Proverbs 22:6)

I feel blessed to be able to say, as did Nephi, that I was "born of goodly parents." It seemed to me that our home was a haven of love where my parents were diligent in teaching the truths of the gospel. I had a very close, special relationship with my mother and have always felt great comfort and security from her love.

When I was seven years old I contracted rheumatic fever. It affected my legs, and I was confined to bed for over a month with instructions to put no weight on my feet. Dad carried me wherever I went, which was never any further than the living room or bathroom.

When I finally recovered and returned to school, I was still plagued with strep throat and was often tired and anemic. As I grew older, I learned to accept the continual leg aches and found that heat was the only thing that stopped the pain.

One night when I was about fifteen, my legs were aching more than usual, so I took an extra hot bath and soaked a long time. Mother had bought a new ointment to relieve muscle aches, and I decided to try it. I applied it all over both of my legs. In a few minutes my legs began to feel hot, and within seconds after this they began to burn as if they were actually on fire. I screamed for my mother. She tried everything she could think of and finally called the doctor. His only solution was time: "In an hour or so the pain will subside." By the time Mother hung up the phone, I felt like screaming, the pain was so intense. After telling me what the doctor had said, she tried to distract me with ridiculous stories. I continued to cry and thrash in my bed, yelling at her to leave me alone. She stayed by my bed, sitting in the dark, and continued with the stories. For a few minutes she had me laughing through my tears, because the stories were so ridiculous. The pain finally eased, and I drifted off to sleep.

I have often reflected on that night, remembering how rude and ungrateful I was for my mother's efforts. It helped me realize that no matter what I did, Mother and Dad would still love me.

The relationship we have with a child may be the most motivating factor in his life. Christ, the greatest example, said of his relationship with his Father in heaven: "I do nothing of myself; but as my Father hath taught me, I speak these things." (John 8:28.) Fathers are prime examples to their sons.

The scriptures contain poignant examples of fathers teaching their sons, such as Lehi (2 Nephi 1–3) and King Benjamin (Mosiah 1:1-8). Alma instructs his son Helaman, "O, remember, my son, and learn wisdom in thy youth; yea, learn in thy youth to keep the commandments of God. . . . Counsel with the Lord in all thy doings." (Alma 37:35, 37.)

One of the greatest challenges and responsibilities a person bears in this life is to guide another, younger life to its full blossom. As parents and teachers, we have a desire to see that young person reach his or her full beauty and glory. We can reach this goal only if we establish loving relationships with our children, and through these relationships effectively influence their lives.

To be effective in their interaction with their children, parents should possess certain traits and abilities. To discover these traits, we can search the scriptures.

"And faith, hope, charity and love, with an eye single to the glory of God, qualify him for the work. Remember faith, virtue, knowledge, temperance, patience, brotherly kindness, godliness, charity, humility, diligence." (D&C 4:5-6; see also Proverbs 31:26; Ephesians 6:4.) Would not these qualifications for missionaries also be desirable in those who guide children? Would parents bringing up their little ones in the light of the gospel want to be any less qualified?

Let's examine these traits and a few others in a little more detail:

1. Faith—confidence in the child
2. Hope—anticipation of growth
3. Love and charity—unconditional feelings
4. Virtue—purity
5. Patience—understanding, long-suffering
6. Knowledge—wisdom
7. Temperance—control of emotions, appetites, and habits
8. Kindness—gentleness, not harshness
9. Godliness—honest example
10. Humility—willingness to admit mistakes, teachability
11. Diligence—caring for physical needs, conscientious effort
12. Forgiveness—compassionate empathy
13. Impartiality—fairness
14. Sense of humor—optimism
15. Consistent discipline—limits and redirection

This list may seem overwhelming, but fortunately children are forgiving, and we as parents don't have to be perfect to succeed—though we should always be aiming toward perfection. We're allowed to lose our tempers and make some mistakes.

Author Judith Viorst asked children, "What's a good mommy?" Their responses were revealing: "A good mommy runs when you get hurt, she doesn't just walk. She doesn't just say, 'Oh no, what is it now?' She thinks it's serious even if you're not bleeding." "And if you fall out of the car while you're driving to see your grandma, she wouldn't scream, 'Stupid, I said not to lean on the door!' She picks you up and makes sure that nothing is broken. And *then* she screams, 'Stupid, I said not to lean on the door!'"

None of the children expected a mother to never get mad. "She has to, or she'll faint from holding it in." "She's allowed to get very, very, very, very mad. If she didn't get mad, she wouldn't be a good mommy, she'd be a dumb mommy."

A good mommy also makes rules about bedtime, and most of the children accept them, "or else you are grouchy and kicky and bitey next day." And though they have dreams of the freedom to eat a hundred ice creams—"more if that's what I want"—they clearly believe a good mother should guard them from stomachaches and cavities and all other hazards of over-indulgence. (Judith Viorst, "What's a Good Mommy," *Redbook,* October 1974, pp. 38-40.)

Christ, the example in all things, said of his relationship with his Father, "The Son can do nothing of himself, but what he seeth the Father do: for what things soever he doeth, these also doeth the Son likewise." (John 5:19.) Ultimately, our individual relationships with our eternal Father in heaven will influence our relationships with our children. When the eternal relationship is strong, we are nourished as parents to likewise develop a loving relationship with our own children. "Beloved, if God so loved us, we ought also to love one another."(1 John 4:11.) What are some principles in establishing a loving relationship?

Principles of a Loving Relationship

1. *Create love and respect.*

Our children learn to love by receiving and feeling love. Love is the foundation for all guidance and the most influential force in the world. Every child needs to feel a close bond of love. We hear a lot about how parents should love their children, but we don't hear much about the great love those children return. The bond of love is expressed mutually in the relationship. The parent is the first to love and to express that love. This is the order of things; as was said of Christ: "We love him, because he first loved us."(1 John 4:19.)

A father tenderly kissed his two-year-old daughter in church. He kissed her ever so softly, barely touching her cheek. He did so about three times, and then the little girl squirmed to get free so she could return the kiss. She kissed him exactly the same way—softly and tenderly. Children return the love they are given, often in much the same way that it was expressed.

Children need to have love expressed to them both in words and in action. Every person needs physical affection. It's easy to give this affection to a baby, because in meeting his needs we have to hold and touch him. Our loving manner in comforting or feeding him does much to build his healthy personality. Some babies are less cuddly and do not want to be held much, which makes it all the more important to give feelings of love when caring for their needs.

One mother expressed this: "I find it important to lovingly touch my children often. It seems to give them great security when I draw them near and hold them as I talk or as they share something with me. I usually have my arm around one child while patting another. It seems this show of affection makes each child feel accepted and loved and an important part of our family circle."

As the child grows older, he still needs physical affection, but his needs change, and the manner of acceptable expression may also change. The eleven- or twelve-year-old boy may resist a kiss from his mother as "mushy," but enjoys roughhousing or wrestling with his father. Mother may need to change her show of affection to a back rub or a hug. Although a teenager may resist affection from his parents, it is vital that he receive it. As he matures, he will not only accept but appreciate and cherish those special moments. Warm, loving touches of affection must start at infancy and never stop.

Respect is an aspect of love that strengthens the parent-child relationship. If the child values our opinion, he will most likely listen to our counsel. When a boy looks up to his father and respects the man that he is, the father's influence becomes powerful. A teenage daughter who respects her father will listen to his lectures even though at times she appears to take them lightly or to brush them off altogether. Later, when a crisis arises, she will be more apt to remember the things he taught.

2. *Recognize individuality.*

Our children will see their own uniqueness as we recognize and accept each one's individuality. The Savior said, "Again, the kingdom of heaven is like unto a net, that was cast into the sea, and gathered of every kind." (Matthew 13:47.)

This scripture indicates that in the Lord's kingdom there is room for people of all kinds. The great variety of the Lord's creations should help us realize more fully that truly the Lord is no respecter of persons.

Each individual wants to be accepted and valued for who he is. The loving relationship involves a basic faith or belief in the dignity and worth of the individual as a unique person. We express trust by accepting the self-expression of others without making value judgments.

Bart was never alone in his play. His exciting ideas and warm, enthusiastic manner continually drew other children to him. Allen, on the other hand, was a slow-moving, quiet boy who seemed more content with his own company, perhaps with one special friend or with toys.

Each child as a unique person must relate to others and to his world in his own way. To build relationships, parents must accept each child as an individual with his own special qualities—Bart with his friendliness and Allen with his quiet serenity. One should not be valued or preferred over the other. That impartiality is difficult to maintain in a family.

Parents of children like Bart and Allen sometimes prefer the gregarious one; it is easier for them to relate to him since he makes life fun and interesting for everyone around. Children like Allen may seem distant, difficult to know, and socially inept. Realizing that children's needs vary according to their individuality, parents should meet those needs with sensitive alertness.

In nursery school, Katherine, an especially lovely little girl, needed and sought much physical affection. When she came to school in the morning, she climbed onto my lap and hugged me. I hugged her back, and then I needed to set out some art materials. Katherine wouldn't let go. I tried to peel her off, but she clung tight. I got up, and she still hung on like a little monkey. I carried her with me for a while, giving her a little squeeze in between taking care of the materials. She would grin and hug me back, but she refused to let go. This happened nearly every day for a week. I would carry her on my hip, and she would wrap her legs around my waist, hugging and smiling at me the whole time. I would squeeze her back and she seemed fine as long as I held her. After a while she seemed more secure and didn't need quite so much affection, but she still had days when she wanted lots of hugs. Katherine's mother said, "She has always been a very cuddly baby and needs more affection than the other children."

After this experience with Katherine, I decided I was not spending enough time with some of the other children. One day I decided to spend more time with Mike. I sat by him at snack time and story time and followed him around as he played, being interested in whatever he did. About halfway through the morning he looked at me and said, "You can go play with the other kids now." He didn't need that much attention; in fact, it was almost smothering to him.

Parents sometimes make mistakes because they fail to treat each child as an individual. Personality responses are different; perceptions are unique. Discipline should be varied according to the needs of the child. Some children respond to verbal correction; others require action. The Doctrine and Covenants records the Lord's responses to individuals according to their needs. He gave instruction according to each person's capacities, both at such a time and in such a manner that the person could understand it.

The Lord told Oliver Cowdery, "Behold, thou knowest that thou hast inquired of me and I did enlighten thy mind; and now I tell thee these things that thou mayest know that thou hast been enlightened by the Spirit of truth." (D&C 6:15.)

In speaking to John Whitmer, the Lord said: "For behold, I speak unto you with sharpness and with power, for mine arm is over all the earth. And I will tell you that which no man knoweth save me and thee alone." (D&C 15:2-3.)

When Joseph Smith was hunted and his life threatened, the Lord gave comfort: "Thy days are known, and thy years shall not be numbered less; therefore, fear not what man can do, for God shall be with you forever and ever." (D&C 122:9.)

These are three of many scriptural examples of the individual help and responses the Lord has given. Parents should be ever alert to the individuality of each child and conscientiously make each feel accepted.

3. *Develop trust.*

Our children will learn trust by observing exemplary models and feeling our trust in them. Parents can foster trust from the time the child is small by giving him small tasks to do and following up to see that he does them. As the child learns, the parent can state, "I can trust you to do this work, and I won't have to remind you to do it." He then gives praise when the job is accomplished.

Allowing the child freedom to make more and more decisions as he grows, and stating confidence in his ability to do so, will also build trust. As he reaches adolescence, his feeling of being trusted will be firmly established. The confidence that comes from trust is especially needed in making the adjustments of adolescence. As children grow and gain independence from their parents and have to make more critical decisions on their own, parents want and should expect them to respond in a trustworthy way, in keeping with the morality and ethics they have been taught. Physical and sexual maturity bring powers of great magnitude, and the adjustments involving these powers are difficult and serious. The trust in the relationship between parent and adolescent can be the most significant and effective influence in helping the teenager to stay close to the values of the family. The youth who feels that his parents trust him will hesitate to do anything that would break that trust.

Bret had been going around with friends who drank and smoked. When his mother complained to him about it, he promised that he would not drink. One night he came home drunk and very sick and said, "Mother, I've got the flu." Each time he threw up, the smell made it very clear to her that he did not have the flu. But she said nothing, and she tenderly nursed him through three days of nausea. Afterward he came to her and said, "You know last week when I was sick, well, I didn't have the flu. I had been drinking and I'm sorry and I'll never do it again." His mother's trust was important to Bret, and this time he kept his promise. Her trust and confidence also made it possible for him to come and talk to her about it.

4. *Establish communication.*

We can establish communication with our children by observing, listening, and then demonstrating our understanding and empathy. As a young child grows and is able to talk, he wants to be listened to. When we listen in order to understand, and then fill his requests, he feels loved and cared for. He trusts our dependability in caring for his needs. As he enters his teens, he especially needs understanding. He is trying all kinds of new ideas and is often quite insistent that he's right on any topic discussed. A parent's patient listening and uncritical response will help keep communication open between them.

Scott came home from school irritated with his friends. As he sat down at the table to have some cookies and milk, he said, "Layne says the new coach at the high school holds more world records in basketball than anyone else even though he is only five-foot-eleven. I think he's wrong; he couldn't do that well. I've watched him coach, and he's not that good."

His mother responded, "Why don't you get your *Guinness Book of World Records* out and check it?"

"I will." Scott left the room and returned with his book. As he read, his mother asked, "Did you find his name at all?"

Scott answered, "Yeah, he has made a few records. Big deal. I still say he's not that good. He must have been a lot younger then."

His mother's uncritical response to Scott's negative,

know-it-all attitude allowed Scott to feel comfortable in talking with her. Although many times she does suggest he find out all the facts before he takes a strong position, she listens enough to keep him talking and communicating with her.

Good communication should be nurtured throughout the years; it is especially critical to maintain during adolescence. The formerly cooperative, obedient youngster overnight seems to become moody and critical of others. He is negative and rebellious about family rules that he accepted earlier. He may become surly, disrespectful, and unreasonable in many ways. The negative behaviors make it very hard for parents to be patient, and they frequently react with anger. If they could instead demonstrate empathy, calmness, and love, they could help the young adolescent feel close to them throughout the difficult adjustments of those years.

The following scripture is an excellent guide for maintaining good communication, especially with teenagers: "Let no corrupt communication proceed out of your mouth, but that which is good to the use of edifying, that it may minister grace unto the hearers." (Ephesians 4:29.)

Teenagers in the process of establishing self-identity are very sensitive to criticism. They need encouragement and genuine praise. Their negative behavior sometimes makes it difficult to find actions to praise, but with effort—sometimes great effort—parents can encourage and build when it is most needed.

5. *Maintain consistency.*

Our relationships with our children will be stronger if they see our actions as dependable and predictable. One of the attributes of God is that he is unchanging, "the same yesterday, today, and forever." (Mormon 9:19.) Consistency in responding to their children's needs is a trait parents should strive for, because inconsistency creates confusion and insecurity. Parents who respond one time with lax discipline and another with firm or even harsh discipline will create instability in their relationship with their children. Because "a double minded man is unstable in all his ways" (James 1:8), the child may think his parents' love for him will waver also. Such wavering may leave him "like a wave of the sea driven with the wind and tossed" (James 1:6) when it comes to the values his parents try to teach.

Consistency, on the other hand, indicates that behavior has predictability about it. It builds confidence and mutual trust. It should be involved in everything from family rules to emotional responses. For example, a parent should not get angry over the late hours one night and then act indifferently another time. Inconsistency can destroy respect.

Consistency is caring. Expressions of love should not be based on whether or not the child achieves in school or sports, but should reflect appreciation of the inherent and constant worth of the child.

Consistency does not imply rigidity. It can exist with flexibility. Consistency that builds trust does not mean that we don't ever change our minds or that we never break a promise or forget to follow through—all parents and teachers have that happen. The kind of consistency that builds trust is the constant and pervasive feeling we communicate that says "I am here for you." "I'm in this world to help you." "I'm here to make your life better." It is communicated not simply in words, but most importantly by constant loving acts of kindness and of giving of oneself. If the child feels that we are responding out of concern and love for him, that all-important trust between us will grow.

The consistent feeling of "I'm here for you, I'm on your side" nurtured the trusting relationship I have with my own mother. As I was growing up, I felt she was always on my side. When there were conflicts in the family and I was hurt, she always took time to explain. When I felt unjustly dealt with, she would listen and talk to me until I understood what had happened and was convinced that the discipline was appropriate. Even if I didn't like it, I understood that it was right. When I needed advice as I grew into adolescence, I would seek counsel from her instead of my friends, because I knew she would not lead me wrong. Out of jealousy or immaturity, my friends sometimes did not give true answers; they were more concerned for themselves. But Mother had *my* interest at heart, and I trusted her opinion over any others. I remember her saying to me once, as I was preparing to leave for college, "If I treat you right, you'll leave me."

I didn't understand at first, but I grew to know that I had to go on into other relationships. My mother loved me enough to encourage that growth, and I trusted her because of it. Our relationship grew deeper because she let me go. She was not jealous of my friends; she knew I needed their association. Parents sometimes have a hard time letting children grow up and move away. They become possessive of those whom they love. Possessiveness limits both persons involved in the relationship.

The consistency that both of my parents offered was that of unending faith in me. When experiences with others left me in shreds, I could go home, and my parents' faith and confidence always put me back together. I could always count on them, and that cemented our relationship.

As our children grow up, our relationships with them are constantly changing. The challenge to keep close to each child is difficult, but it pays great dividends. As we as parents have that special closeness wherein the child feels our love and returns it, both our lives and his life become richer and happier. We enjoy the rewards of seeing him find success and happiness amid all his struggles, and we ourselves find success and happiness in him.

The relationships we have with our children have enduring value in life. Ultimately, as we each develop a deeper and closer relationship with our Father in heaven, we can become more effective with our own children and develop a deeper relationship with each of them.

Chapter 2

Listen and Communicate

Wherefore, he that preacheth and he that
receiveth, understand one another, and both
are edified and rejoice together.
(D&C 50:22)

Do we truly listen to each other? Do we hear the silent plea behind the words of a child who asks: "What are you doing? What's that for? How does it work?" Do we know when "I can't" really means "I'm afraid"? Do we understand the feelings of jealousy in the words "He thinks he's so smart"? Do we realize the hurt in "You never believe me," or "You always let him be first"? Do we recognize the impending explosion in "If someone doesn't come and help me, I'm going to scream"? Do we hear the fear in "How long will you be gone, and when will you come back to get me"?

Are we tuned in to what our children are trying to tell us? Do we take time to hear the silent messages? Do we teach them to only half-listen to us, as we only half-listen to them? Does our inattention to them teach them to develop poor listening habits? Do we give them the same respectful listening ear that we give our peers or leaders?

Much happy human interaction is based on mutual

understanding. Real effort, patience, and selflessness are required in listening to and understanding another human heart. Sound principles based upon the scriptures can aid us in listening to and communicating effectively with our children.

Section 1 of the Doctrine and Covenants, the Lord's preface to the doctrines, covenants, and commandments revealed in this dispensation, emphasizes the vital role of listening. "Hearken, O ye people of my church, saith the voice of him who dwells on high, and whose eyes are upon all men; yea, verily I say: Hearken ye people from afar; and ye that are upon the islands of the sea, *listen together.*" (D&C 1:1; italics added.)

The Lord says, in essence, "Sit up and take note and *listen.* This is important." He warns us to be prepared to listen and learn from the instructions and commandments that follow.

In our goals to be better parents and leaders of children, we must attune ourselves to listening carefully before we try to guide. First we listen to learn and understand; then we are in a position to effectively guide our children.

Principles of Effective Listening and Communicating

1. *Listen with love.*

By showing genuine love and concern in listening to our children, we increase our influence in our relationships with them. Loving others, the second greatest commandment (see Mark 12:31), can be accomplished by genuinely listening.

Jesus listened to and was especially loving and protective of children. He said, "Suffer little children to come unto me, and forbid them not: for of such is the kingdom of God." (Luke 18:16.) His love for little children was also recorded in the Book of Mormon in his visit to the Nephites after his crucifixion. "He commanded that their little children should be brought." He knelt down in the midst of the children with the multitude and prayed, and all received unspeakable joy, after which "he took their little children, one by one, and blessed them, and prayed unto the Father for them." (See 3 Nephi 17:11-24.) Contemplating that scene would swell the hearts of most parents.

As we listen to our children, we can extend love to them by having a noncritical, nonjudging attitude. That may be easy when they are quite young, but when they reach adolescence, it can become difficult. "Condemn me not because of mine imperfection" (Mormon 9:31) is a cry we all might echo.

Some parents have the mistaken idea that acceptance means condoning; they fail to distinguish between the two. One can accept feelings and behavior without giving sanction or approval. For example, suppose our daughter hits her younger brother when he grabs her new toy. We can say, "I know you are angry" (this is acceptance), "but I can't allow you to hit him" (and not condoning). We need to recognize how our child feels and to express to him our understanding of his feelings, without allowing destructive behavior to continue.

As we teach our children the gospel, and do so with a listening heart, we can become "humble, meek, submissive, patient, full of love." (Alma 13:28.)

2. *Read nonverbal messages to gain insight.*

By recognizing nonverbal messages from our children, we will gain insight into the real meaning behind their words. Helaman's son Nephi exercised this kind of discernment when he told some disbelievers how to recognize a murderer they sought: "And then shall he tremble, and shall look pale, even as if death had come upon him. And then shall ye say: Because of this fear and this paleness which has come upon your face, behold, we know that thou art guilty." (Helaman 9:33-34.)

Sometimes outward physical expression is more revealing than words. This is especially true with children.

Examples in the scriptures indicate that the feelings of the heart—both righteousness and wickedness—are exposed in the face. Cain let his anger change his heart: "And Cain was very wroth, and his countenance fell. And the Lord said unto Cain, Why art thou wroth? and why is thy countenance fallen?" (Genesis 4:5-6.)

Isaiah declares of the wicked, "The show of their countenance doth witness against them, and doth declare their sin to be even as Sodom, and they cannot hide it." (2 Nephi 13:9.) Contrary to sin, we read in Proverbs, "A merry heart maketh a cheerful countenance." (Proverbs 15:13.) The Nephites showed their righteousness when Christ appeared and taught them. They became converted and "were as white as the countenance . . . of Jesus." (3 Nephi 19:25.)

We should remember, as we study these scriptures, that countenance involves more than just physical appearance. Countenance is defined as expressions of "the face as an indication of mood, emotion, or character." *(Webster's New Collegiate Dictionary,* p. 259.) Observing the countenance of a child when we listen will certainly help us understand.

As adults, we often rely too much on a child's words alone to give us direction for our responses to him. In doing so, we tend to forget the limitations of his verbal skills. Children do not always have the words at their command to express how they feel, so they of necessity use their bodies. We need to observe more closely what the child's behavior is trying to communicate.

Dan, the oldest of seven children, was a responsible and sober boy. Then he began acting silly and rude, which was not natural for him. At times he became irritable, but when he was asked about it, he didn't respond. One hint came when he said he didn't like school. When asked why, he replied, "Just don't." When his mother consulted with his teacher, she learned that he was doing poorly in reading. As she talked to Dan about his reading, he seemed very self-conscious and embarrassed. But when he received extra help, his reading skills improved and the silly, rude, self-conscious behavior disappeared.

Many times children cannot say exactly what is bothering them. They may not even know. But we can learn to know the personality of each child well enough to sense the deeper or hidden meanings in what he says. This understanding expands our perception of his needs and increases our ability to influence his behavior.

3. *Use plain and simple terms.*

Speaking in plain, simple language on our children's level of understanding can lead to successful communication. Nephi's instruction as to how the Lord communicated with his people provides an example for us: "For my soul delighteth in plainness; for after this manner doth the Lord God work among the children of men. For the Lord God giveth light unto the understanding; for he speaketh unto men according to their language, unto their understanding." (2 Nephi 31:3.) If we follow this scriptural example, we will gear our communication with our children to their level of understanding.

When the church was restored, this same principle was used. "These commandments are of me, and were given unto my servants in their weakness, after the manner of their language, that they might come to understanding." (D&C 1:24.)

Our communication with our children should be in relation to their actual experience. In telling a child it will soon be time to leave, we can generate better understanding and therefore more willing obedience if we say, "You will be able to ride your trike to the corner and back two more times before it is time to leave." This will make much more sense to him than "You have five more minutes to play."

Jesus, the Master Teacher, talked about the wind,

waves, seeds, trees, and other things with which the people had experience to help them understand. (See Matthew 13; Luke 13.) And so with our children, we will have better success when we communicate with them using "words easy to be understood" (1 Corinthians 14:9) that relate to their previous experience.

My three-and-a-half-year-old son, Randy, asked, "Where do people go when they die?" I had explained earlier, when his younger sister, Laura, was born, that she had lived with Heavenly Father before she came to live with us. I said, "She came down from heaven to live with us, and if she should die, she would go back to Heavenly Father. When someone dies, they go back to Heavenly Father." Randy seemed content with that answer. In his play a few days later, as he pretended to rescue his dog from his bath water, he said, "Oh dear, he's dead. He's not here any more; he got born up to Jesus."

If we will do with our children as the Lord does with us, "reasoning in plainness and simplicity" (D&C 133:57), we will establish warm communication and thereby give them understanding and guide their lives.

4. *Keep confidences.*

Keeping the confidences of our children can strengthen our relationships with them. "A talebearer revealeth secrets: but he that is of a faithful spirit concealeth the matter." (Proverbs 11:13.) This scripture makes it clear that a wise parent will keep faith with his children by honoring confidential communications.

The principle of confidentiality is aimed at maintaining respect by showing consideration. We all make mistakes, and this principle, if followed, can make it easier to repent.

In Matthew 18:15, we read: "If thy brother shall trespass against thee, go and tell him his fault between thee and him alone: if he shall hear thee, thou hast gained thy brother." (See also D&C 42:88.) The Lord has elaborated on this idea in modern scriptures: "If any shall offend in secret, he or she shall be rebuked in secret, that he or she may have opportunity to confess in secret to him or her whom he or she has offended, and to God, that the church may not speak reproachfully of him or her." (D&C 42:92; see also 28:11; 42:89.)

No truly repentant sinner wants to be remembered for his sins. Children also feel embarrassed by their wrongdoings, and our keeping their mistakes private allows them to have more self-respect, and perhaps could make it easier for them to overcome the problem.

The principle of keeping confidences applies not only when repentance is necessary, but also in other aspects of a relationship. When a child confides some trivial matter that to him is serious, we cause great hurt when we laughingly tell a neighbor who later recalls the matter to him. After such betrayal, confidence is hard to win back. Every child needs to know that the things he tells his parents are kept in confidence. The small yet traumatic experience that seems so dramatic to a child needs to be given respect. Although to us it is really humorous—or at least not serious—it is best to receive it with the concern with which it was given.

If a child comes to us confiding some fear that he has and we say, "Don't be silly, there is nothing to be afraid of," he will probably keep other feelings to himself in the future. By accepting the feelings and ideas he expresses, we show respect for him as a person.

Parents can shelter children from embarrassing situations. When Bob had an accident and wet the bed, his thoughtful mother quietly changed the sheets without saying a word to anyone, and said privately in an attitude of kind helpfulness, "Bob, do you want me to get you up tonight?" When a child sees his mother keeping his embarrassment secret, he then feels he can trust her with more serious problems later.

5. *Ask questions to express interest and to teach.*

As we ask our children questions, we show interest in

them and teach new perspectives and ideas. Questioning can be used to teach, add insight, and provoke deep thought. Jesus, a master in every way, often used questions to teach. When asked a question, he frequently answered with another question. His response when he was taken before Pilate is a good example. Pilate asked him, "Art thou the King of the Jews?" Jesus replied, "Sayest thou this thing of thyself, or did others tell it thee of me?" (John 17:33-34.) Another example is given following the Resurrection when his disciples saw and talked with him, and Peter, seeing John following Jesus, said, "Lord, and what shall this man do?" Jesus replied, "If I will that he tarry till I come, what is that to thee?" (John 21:21-22.) The disciples had been somewhat jealous of one another as to who should be the greatest among them. This question was almost a chastisement to Peter. The Savior's soul-searching questions provoked deeper thinking, better understanding, and greater insight.

We also can more effectively teach our children if we will make wise use of questions asked in an appropriate way. Questions work especially well with teenagers if they are used to replace the usual blanket statements or direct commands. Suppose we have established that our teenager is to vacuum the basement and do the ironing each Friday. From past experience we know that Friday may come and go with the work remaining undone. A gentle reminder in the form of a question, "Will you have time to do the ironing today?" will be less offensive and more committal than the direct order, such as, "Be sure to do the ironing today," or "Don't forget you have to do your work today." Because teenagers are going through a time of finding their independence, questions are more effective in giving direction and causing them to think more deeply.

Suppose a young man is trying to decide whether to go on a mission when he turns nineteen or to complete another year of college first. His parents want him to go at nineteen. They have seen young men who postpone their missions and ended up getting married instead, or who became so involved in school or other interests that they ultimately decided not to go on missions. Rather than try to convince him of the choice they want him to make by stating the reasons why he should go soon, they might pose some questions to help him think of the consequences of each alternative:

"How many boys who postpone a mission end up getting married instead?" "What is your purpose in waiting a year?" "Will waiting move you closer to a mission, or will it involve you in things that will incline you away from a mission?" "What are your long-range goals?" "What are the risks of each choice in attaining your goals?" "Does one choice contain more risks than the other?"

Such questions, offered in an attitude of helpfulness, will help him use wisdom in making his choice. The parents have offered the guidance he needed. They may feel it necessary to be directive later, but they should first use the questions to see if he won't of his own accord make the better choice.

Our using questions when children are young and throughout their growing years can help them arrive at adolescence with good decision-making skills that lead gradually but surely to healthy independence.

6. *Give equal opportunity to be heard.*

As we give our children equal opportunity to be heard, their feelings of self-worth will be increased. The order that should be established in our communication is stated in this verse from the Doctrine and Covenants: "And let not all be spokesmen at once; but let one speak at a time and let all listen unto his sayings, that when all have spoken that all may be edified of all, and that every man may have an equal privilege." (D&C 88:122.)

The principle of showing respect and equality in speaking and listening can be used to improve communications in the family. If we establish the attitude of listening to each one of our children, we can create feelings of mutual consideration. Our example will encourage brothers and sisters to listen to each other. This in turn can be conducive to having the Spirit of the Lord in our homes.

In one young family a special aunt came to visit. The children were excited and all wanted to tell her something, and their attempts escalated into a low roar. Finally she said, "Let me listen to Jimmy, and then I will hear what each of you has to say." They became quiet. In a few minutes, however, they were all shouting again, all wanting to talk at once. Jimmy turned to the others and said, "She's listening to Cathy; she'll listen to you in a minute." As the children grew in confidence that each would indeed have a turn, there was less shouting and more patience.

We need to give our children the assurance that each will have a turn to talk while the others listen. When this order is established and children do have their turn to talk, they grow in their feelings of belonging to the family and in their interest in others' points of view.

Perhaps the most difficult part of listening for some parents is the time involved. In telling their stories or relating experiences children often lose their train of thought. Patience and perhaps even prompting are necessary to give them practice in organizing and expressing themselves.

Not only do children often pick inappropriate times for demanding our listening ear, but sometimes they seem to want more time than we have to give. We can't always set aside other demands to give our undivided attention for an extended time. When we say, "In a minute, dear," and do not forget, but go in a few moments to listen and see, the child is reassured that he is not forgotten. When it is necessary for us to do other things, such as prepare dinner, we can simply take our child by the hand

and lead him to the kitchen with an assuring, "Yes, continue. I want to keep listening." We can comment on the child's story while we prepare the meal (or do other tasks), thus not breaking his conversational train of thought.

As long as there are times when the child has our undivided attention, when we are fully concentrating on him, even if only for five minutes at a stretch, he will then be understanding when we need to combine our listening with other responsibilities or even put him off until later.

One father took frequent short business trips that sometimes involved staying overnight in a motel. When possible, he invited one of his six children to go with him. As they traveled, he catered to the desires of that child. The eldest liked to eat at nice restaurants. The youngest liked to buy lots of goodies and eat all along the way. Each child looked forward to his turn to go with their father, and there was always time to talk and to listen. Communication skills were developed, relationships were strengthened, and memories were created.

We should be diligent in providing an atmosphere wherein each child has the opportunity to be heard, to grow in verbal ability, and to develop a feeling of self-importance.

7. *Listen to the promptings of the Spirit.*

The Lord will guide us if we will only be humble and listen. The Holy Ghost is given to us to teach us, but sensitivity and real listening are necessary if we are to hear a "still small voice." (See 1 Kings 19:11-12; 1 Nephi 17:45.)

As our children proceed through life, the whisperings of the Holy Spirit can be a source of strength and direction to help us guide them past danger points. The Spirit will help us know not only what to do but also, if necessary, when and how to do it. (See 2 Nephi 32:5; D&C 100:2; 136:33.) It takes faith and trust in the Lord to follow the Spirit's promptings. It is possible, if we are faithful like Nephi, for us to be led completely by the Spirit, "not knowing beforehand" what should be done. (See 1 Nephi 4:6.) Our children need to know that we guide them with promptings from the Holy Spirit.

Sometimes we may be led to do things that seem unusual or irrational, but we have been given this counsel and its promise: "Trust in the Lord with all thine heart; and lean not unto thine own understanding. In all thy ways acknowledge him, and he shall direct thy paths." (Proverbs 3:5-6.)

As a young teenager, I wanted to attend a party, but my mother advised me not to go. When I asked why not, she said, "I just have a feeling that you shouldn't go." That was not a good enough reason for me, so I went anyway. At the party there was drinking, profanity, and I saw some ugly, immoral behavior that I wish I had never seen. Those scenes later haunted me, and I deeply regretted having gone to the party. After this experience, I knew that when Mother was "tuned in," I had better listen to her. She never said, "I have a feeling," unless she felt prompted by the Spirit.

One man said, "My mother guided me through the promptings of the Holy Ghost all of my life. Whenever I had a fight with my brother or was angry at someone at school or resentful of something I had to do, my mother seemed to know ahead of time and would draw me aside and say, 'I want to talk with you.'" He said he couldn't remember what she had said in those situations, but he always felt better afterward. If he had been angry at his brother, he didn't feel angry anymore, or, at least, he felt more at peace.

Once as a teenager he became angry when his mother said again, "I want to talk with you," and he responded, "I've listened to you all my life, and I'm not going to listen any more." After he cooled down, he began to wonder what she had been going to say. He went to her and asked, "What were you going to say, Mother?" She answered, "I don't know. The Spirit won't tell me now."

He said he learned a great lesson from his mother's example and from the scriptures about how the Spirit guides: "Neither take ye thought beforehand what ye shall say; but treasure up in your minds continually the words of life, and it shall be given you in the very hour." (D&C 84:85.) "For it shall be given you in the very hour, yea, in the very moment, what ye shall say." (D&C 100:6.)

As parents entrusted with the vital, sacred responsibility of teaching and rearing children, we should ever humbly and diligently strive to be worthy to receive the daily promptings of the Holy Spirit as we build our families. If we record spiritual experiences while they are fresh, they become testimonies to our children of our faithfulness. As children grow into that difficult teenage period, we can refer back to the record of these promptings and let our teenagers read them, thus giving reinforcement to our guidance as well as creating in them reassurance and confidence in our wisdom.

As we listen, as the scripture suggests, "with real intent" (Moroni 10:4), we might ask: Do I focus my attention and keep my eyes on my child as I listen? Do I watch his eyes to see whether they dart about in anxiety, or seem clouded and troubled or turn almost inward in search of himself? Do I notice the total expression of his face and the way his words flow? Do I listen carefully to the tone of his voice, remembering that the tone quality will often tell more than the words? Do I hear the gay tones of a heart on the wings of joy, or the low, mournful sounds of a troubled soul? Do I watch to see what he does with his hands? Do I observe the tenseness in his body and watch it relax as I let him talk on? In essence, do I give my whole heart and attention in an effort to understand? Do I let him know of my understanding?

When we listen with such intensity, we can reap the rewards of real depth in love and understanding with our children. We can also learn from them, for "little children do have words given unto them many times, which confound the wise and the learned." (Alma 32:23.)

Chapter 3

Give Encouragement

Pleasant words are as an honeycomb,
sweet to the soul, and health to the bones.
(Proverbs 16:24)

If we followed the example we read in the scriptures, we would use encouragement extensively. "Withhold not good from them to whom it is due, when it is in the power of thine hand to do it." (Proverbs 3:27.) As children grow, they need inspiration and hope just as flowers need sun. Some child psychologists believe that a child misbehaves mainly because he is discouraged, and that parents would encounter less misbehavior in their youngsters if they used more encouragement.

Principles of Encouragement

1. *Set realistic expectations.*

We can encourage our children by setting expectations that are within their ability to perform. This principle is mentioned in several places in the scriptures. In speaking to Joseph Smith regarding translation, the Lord said, "Do not run faster or labor more than you have strength . . . but be diligent unto the end." (D&C

10:4.) In the process of restoring the gospel, the Lord said in tenderness, "Behold, ye are little children and ye cannot bear all things now; ye most grow in grace and in the knowledge of the truth." (D&C 50:40.)

As we try to encourage our children, we will not go amiss if we use this same tenderness that Christ has shown to us. We can nurture our children's growth in any area if we set realistic expectations. It will quickly discourage a child who is expected to act and perform as a four-year-old if he is barely three.

Jim, who was one year older than his brother Sam, was nimble and quick in dressing himself. But Sam was as large as Jim, and the subtle expectations of their parents said to him, "You're as big as Jim, and you should be able to do it just as well and as quickly as he does." As the boys were preparing to go outside one morning, Jim quickly put on his clothes while Sam cried and stormed around and said he couldn't find his shoe. He had begun to expect of himself what his parents had implied. His failure to measure up caused many tears and frustrations for him. His mother, finally realizing what was happening, said, "I keep forgetting he's a whole year younger and needs more assistance."

Fulfilling expectations that are within his capabilities can give a child a sense of worth and accomplishment. Those set far beyond his reach lead to frustration and discouragement.

Comparisons can be frustrating to the child. Think how defeating it could be to have a parent say, "See how well Jim did on his grades. You should do as well." The child inwardly says, "But I'm not Jimmy. Why do you want me to be like him? Does that mean that I'm not as worthwhile in your eyes as Jimmy if I'm not like him? Why can't I just be me?"

While avoiding unrealistic expectations, parents and teachers should be alert to the child's growing capacities. As his capabilities grow, the adults should increase the expectation to keep pace. This encourages continual effort and movement toward higher achievement. They should be reevaluating continually, through sensitive awareness of the child's growth, to properly set expectations that are within his reach. This reevaluation helps the child to be realistic in his efforts and to strive continually upward.

Children need to be taught to have patience with themselves and their growing abilities. As four-year-old Laurie and her teacher sat at the puzzles, Laurie pulled out a puzzle and dumped it out. That particular puzzle was so difficult that even the teacher had trouble with it, and she had planned to put it away. Laurie struggled with it for a minute and then said, "This one is too hard." The teacher said, "Yes, I think that one belongs to the five-year-old group. You'll be able to do it next year. You may put it back if you wish." Laurie slid it back in the box and pulled out another. After she had completed it, she smiled. The teacher commented, "You enjoyed that one, didn't you?" Laurie said, "Yes! That's a fun one!"

When children encounter tasks that are too difficult for them, we can encourage them by expressing confidence in their growing abilities: "When you are a little older and larger, you will be able to do that." As we use this principle with our children, we can hope to be able to say of them as they mature, "They did all labor, every man according to his strength." (Alma 1:26.)

2. *Pace the learning.*

Our children will be encouraged in their performance of particular tasks if we present them in small segments, one step at a time. As we study the restoration of the gospel, we see that the truths and the Church organization were not presented all at once. As Joseph and others gained knowledge, pondered a facet of the gospel, such as the priesthood, and asked the Lord regarding it, the Lord then revealed and restored it to the earth. (See D&C 13; 27:12-13.)

Because this principle of "line upon line, precept upon precept" (2 Nephi 28:30; D&C 98:12) seems the obvious way to teach, it is sometimes overlooked. When children become discouraged, it may be because they are required to deal with too much too fast. If they stop trying, it is usually because the steps are too large or too small, and we may need to reevaluate. We will stimulate better performance from our children by pacing the tasks to their abilities.

Wade, who was large for his age, was uncoordinated and had difficulty with speech. When presented with a task, he would work on it for a minute and then push it away with the comment, "I can't." He was pressured from home to perform, and the pressure served only to frustrate him. At school we were doing some prereading matching games. Wade looked at his paper, scribbled on it, and said, "I can't do it." Then he got up to leave.

I took him gently by the arm, led him back to the table, and said, "I'm sure you can do it. I'll help you." I covered all but the first picture on the paper and asked him to find the number to match the number of flowers in the first square. He pointed to it, and I said, "Good! That's correct. Now draw a line from the square to the number." He did so. "That's right. I knew you could do it. Let's try the next one." By looking at the problems individually, he was able to match each one, whereas looking at the whole paper seemed overwhelming to him.

It may be unwise to outline an entire task to the child all at once. Rather, we should present it one step at a time. When the first step is completed, we can then introduce the next part of the job. This allows us to reward at each step and to plan a rest or a break between steps.

Dad wants Jim to help weed the garden. He takes Jim with him and they work together weeding one row. When that row is completed, Dad says, "My, that looks fine. Let's have a cool lemonade." After finishing their drink they go back to the garden and Dad says, "When this row is done, let's have a cookie." The child is spurred on. Upon completing the third row, Dad says, "Now we can take a five-minute rest under the tree." As they relax in the cool shade, Dad says, "Thanks a lot, Jim. I enjoy working with you. You are a good, steady worker and stay with a job until it is done."

If the father were to show the child the garden and say, "We need to weed the garden," the child would look at that huge weed patch, see a burdensome task, and want to quit before he started. Of course, it is even more discouraging when Dad simply says, "Go weed the garden." Adults often say, "I get tired just thinking about it," when envisioning some gigantic task. How much easier it is to take things one step at a time, "here a little and there a little." (2 Nephi 28:30.)

Children often become discouraged and frustrated with their lack of ability. Pacing the beginning stages of learning will minimize discouragement and increase motivation and performance. As parents and teachers, we can encourage children greatly if we will assist with the same loving tone Jesus used when he said, "Ye cannot bear all things now; nevertheless, be of good cheer, for I will lead you along." (D&C 78:18.)

3. *Offer material rewards.*

By using material rewards, we can stimulate greater effort and achievement until our children learn to value behavior in and of itself. It may be difficult for some parents to see how this principle can produce good results. They remember all too well the scriptures that say, "It is easier for a camel to go through the eye of a needle, than for a rich man to enter into the kingdom of God" (Matthew 19:24), and "Lay not up for yourselves treasures upon earth . . . but lay up for yourselves treasures in heaven. . . . For where your treasure is, there will your heart be also" (Matthew 6:19-21). Some parents feel that material rewards can become bribes and may teach the child to do the right thing for the wrong reason.

If we study the scriptures carefully, we see that the Lord does offer the righteous "for their reward the good things of the earth." (D&C 59:3.) Following his example, we can use material rewards as good incentives for righteous behavior. As imperfect people in somewhat the beginning stages of growth, our children may need such rewards as motivation until the behavior itself becomes satisfying.

Material rewards may include food, candy, toys, money, points, or tokens that can be traded for other things after performance of a desired behavior. When I was a child my parents would pay us for doing little extra jobs other than our regular chores around the house. I recall my older brother Blaine discussing (some would have called it bargaining) with my mother the amount to be paid for a particular job. It seemed at the time, and as we grew, that he was developing an attitude of materialism and would not do anything without knowing how much he would get paid.

The year I graduated from high school, my parents went to Europe to meet my oldest brother, Bill, when he was released from his mission. They planned to travel together before returning home. That left the four of us at home to take care of things while they were away. Although Diane was the oldest, Blaine was the oldest priesthood holder in the house and was "in charge." As the time drew near for our parents to return, Blaine informed the rest of us that we should get the place looking in tip-top shape. During the next week we washed all the windows inside and out, cleaned and waxed the floors, got the root beer off the kitchen ceiling, mowed the lawn, clipped around the flower beds, cleaned the garage, and washed the back porch.

A carpenter working on the house next door commented that he couldn't believe a group of kids would work so hard when their parents weren't even in town. The greatest reward was the satisfaction of seeing the place look so great and the look on Mom's face as she walked around our shining house saying, "Everything looks so beautiful . . . so beautiful!" Blaine had instigated the project with no thoughts of monetary reward.

The Lord has said, "The riches of the earth are mine to give" (D&C 38:39), and our children can be taught that he wants us to have all the good things of the earth if we can handle them in righteousness. The riches that the earth can produce were "ordained for the use of man for food and for raiment, and that he might have in abundance." (D&C 49:19.)

The Church uses awards to stimulate achievement and participation in certain activities. Scouting, Duty to God, and personal achievement awards are given to individuals to encourage diligent, organized effort. When discouragement comes, as it usually does, the thought of the award can stimulate a youth in persistence when he may otherwise drift into an it-doesn't-matter attitude. In the process, he learns the intrinsic value of his Church activity, and the award becomes incidental. With continued effort come maturity and feelings of true devotion. Material rewards can get the child over that little hump that otherwise might be a stumbling block.

With the use of material rewards, we can teach that "the hand of the diligent maketh rich" (Proverbs 10:4), but that we want our children to know the wisdom of Jacob's words: "Before ye seek for riches, seek ye for the kingdom of God. And after ye have obtained a hope in Christ ye shall obtain riches, if ye seek them; and ye will seek them for the intent to do good." (Jacob 2:18-19.)

4. *Be specific in giving praise.*

When praising our children, if we are exact in what we say, our comments will be more meaningful and more helpful.

A father had a chat with his son Jim's Sunday School teacher, who commented that Jim's reverent attitude helped create a reverent tone in his class. Because his father praised Jim for his good example in class, Jim will be encouraged to continue such behavior. Being specific does take more energy and effort from the parent, but it is much more effective in guiding and directing the child's progress.

Not only can we praise behavior, but there are also times when specific praise of a personality trait is appropriate. When a child's behavior says that he is growing in consideration for others, we can encourage him by first praising his specific considerate action and then explaining that the behavior shows him to be a considerate person. Praise of personality mixed with praise of behavior can help a child see where his behavior is leading him.

On one occasion I was working with a boy named Patrick who had entered the preschool group late in the year. Personality differences surfaced immediately between Maryanne, my co-teacher, and Patrick. The day before Patrick was to leave us to enter another school, I sat down and drew him close and said, "Patrick, you will be going to another school soon, and I'm sure you will do fine. You are a smart boy, and you can get along with anyone. You will make friends with the children and the teacher in that new school because you know how to get along with people. You felt that Maryanne has been hard on you, but you got along with her just the same. You didn't like Wade much. He made you angry sometimes, but you let him play with you anyway, and you have learned to have fun with him."

Patrick made no comment. He just smiled and nodded as I talked. I continued, "Yes, you will do very well because you are a smart boy and you can get along with people, even people you don't like. You have learned to be patient and tolerant of almost everyone you know. I'm very happy you've learned those things, and I'm sure you will do well in that new school." Patrick really had made great progress in getting along with others, and I wanted him to know that before he left.

We find many examples in the scriptures when the Lord used specific praise. For example, in the Doctrine and Covenants we read: "Blessed is my servant Hyrum Smith; for I, the Lord, love him because of the integrity of his heart, and because he loveth that which is right before me." (D&C 124:15; see also Luke 8:48; 10:42.)

Being specific in praise is particularly helpful when a child has made a mistake and feels he might not succeed again. When Joseph Smith lost the manuscript of the first part of the Book of Mormon, the Lord first chastized him but then said, "But remember, God is merciful; therefore, repent . . . and thou art still chosen, and art again called to the work." (D&C 3:10.)

5. *Utilize group resources.*

Teaching our children to share their personal strengths for the benefit of others will encourage usefulness and unselfishness. Every child has something special to offer in the family circle. "For there are many gifts, and to every man is given a gift by the Spirit of God. To some is given one, and to some is given another, that all may be profited thereby. . . . To some is given, by the Spirit of God, the word of wisdom. To another is given the word of knowledge, that all may be taught to be wise and to have knowledge. And again, to some it is given to have faith to be healed; and to others it is given to have faith to heal." (D&C 46:11-12, 17-20.)

As I read this scripture, I extend the message to include personality traits. One child may have a cheerful nature and lend much joy to the family; another has great patience and is a calming influence.

A wise parent or teacher will be aware of the strength of each child and use it in ways to assist the optimal development of the other children. As we work and live together, it should be our goal to shed forth our light and to share our abilities to the benefit of those around us. The Lord said, "Let your light so shine before men, that they may see your good works, and glorify your Father which is in heaven." (Matthew 5:16.) An alert parent can guide children to build and grow from each other's strengths.

Becky, an especially flighty, nervous, and excitable child, had difficulty in completing tasks and was easily frustrated. Lynda, on the other hand, was unusually patient and stable. While Becky was playing with the Lego set (small interlocking building blocks), she became angry because she couldn't build as fast as the other children. She knocked over her small pile, saying, "I can't do it."

I suggested that Lynda help Becky. She approached Becky and said, "Let's build one together."

Becky seemed pleased until she noticed that Lynda's wall was getting a little higher than her own. "I can't do it," she said, and started to leave. Lynda responded, "Don't go. You put one on, and then I'll put one on." As Becky struggled to get a block to fit, Lynda patiently watched and waited. "Okay, now I'll put mine on," she said, as she added one to her wall. "Okay, Becky, you put another one on."

Lynda waited again as they took turns adding to their structure. She never hurried Becky or seemed anxious for her own turn. As a result, Becky became more subdued and functioned with better control and greater tolerance for herself.

6. *Be present on important occasions.*

We can encourage our children to develop their talents and other abilities by being in attendance as they perform. The physical presence of one who cares can be a great strengthening force for any individual. When the hour of atonement was drawing near, Jesus took Peter and the two sons of Zebedee to a place called Gethsemane. He asked of them, "Tarry ye here, and watch with me." When he returned from praying, he found them asleep, and said, "Could ye not watch with me one hour?" (Matthew 26:36-40.) How much more en-

couraging it would have been for Jesus had they watched
and not fallen asleep. Jesus, the example for us in all
things, helps us to realize the strengthening influence of
the presence of others.

As our children grow, they will be called upon to perform before others. This can be a very frightening experience. The encouraging presence of parents can help
a child put forth his best effort and can comfort him
should he not do well.

One six-year-old who was participating with his family in giving a spiritual presentation in church faltered
and burst into tears when the time came for his short talk.
His father stepped forward and gently encouraged him
through it. When it was over and they were leaving the
stand, the boy said to his father, "It's nice to have a pal
help out when you need him. I help you out sometimes,
huh, Dad?"

Our children will feel loved as important members of
our family circle if, whenever possible, we support them
by our presence when they have to perform before
others.

Our Father in heaven knows how vital it is for each of
us to have support from others. Joseph Smith was
blessed to have his family's support in all he did. The
Lord provided additional support by commanding
Oliver Cowdery, "Stand by my servant Joseph, faithfully,
in whatsoever difficult circumstances he may be for the
word's sake." (D&C 6:18.)

Some may not be blessed with family support, particularly those who join the Church as converts, but as
Latter-day Saint parents, we can make certain by our
own commitment that our children feel encouragement
and strength from us.

7. *Teach trust in the Lord.*

Our children will find great encouragement in the
scriptures if they are taught from their youth to read and
to believe in them. When a child has developed a tes-

timony that the Lord does stand by what he says, he will be fortified against any of life's vicissitudes. If we teach our children to trust in the Lord and believe all his words, then when they read, "Search diligently, pray always, and be believing, and all things shall work together for your good" (D&C 90:24), they may feel that, with the help of the Lord, they can accomplish any goal.

As Pete began his schooling, he set his goal to become a doctor, though there were no doctors in his family, and his family did not have the finances to help him. After he served a mission, completed his bachelor's degree, and applied for medical school, Pete wondered if he could achieve his goal. He was in love with a wonderful, worthy young woman, and he wanted very much to get married. His parents, however, said they would not help him in medical school if he got married.

Pete felt strongly about getting married, so he decided to go ahead. After he was accepted in medical school and received a scholarship, his parents softened and helped as much as they could. He had trusted in the Lord, and although he didn't know how it could be accomplished, he proceeded to do what he felt was right. The Lord truly did provide means for him to be successful.

The trust we instill in our children can help them realize that "with God all things are possible" (Mark 10:27), and they can live to fulfill the vision of life the Lord has for them. Rearing children with encouragement and praise can be a joyful way to live. Their lives are more apt to be happy and fulfilling if they are given positive praise and support throughout their growth.

Chapter 4

Overcoming Discouragement

For after much tribulation come the blessings.
Wherefore the day cometh that ye
shall be crowned with much glory;
the hour is not yet, but is nigh at hand.
(D&C 58:4)

Most children at some time become discouraged with themselves. They may even feel as Nephi did when he said, "O wretched man that I am! Yea, my heart sorroweth because of my flesh; my soul grieveth because of mine iniquities." (2 Nephi 4:17.) We know that Nephi was a righteous man, and yet, like us all, he occasionally became discouraged with his own performance.

Discouragement may bring thoughts of failure, lack of ability, or worthlessness. The immobility brought on by discouragement should perhaps cause the greatest concern. Children may seem stymied and frustrated, as if all their efforts result only in futility. When such feelings come, they may lapse into a state of doing nothing, and in that lies the great detriment of discouragement.

Because of their limited experience, children constantly face new and different challenges. Thus they need to be taught ways to overcome discouragement. Much is lost if we allow our children to remain in a discouraged state of unhappy immobility. We can best help children fight discouragement if we teach them an eternal perspective of the purpose of life. If we can teach them to perceive and react to their disappointments with a view that "all these things shall give thee experience, and shall be for thy good" (D&C 122:7), they will be less apt to become discouraged and more likely to find the courage to deal with life and its challenges.

Principles in Overcoming Discouragement

1. *Recall past achievements.*

We may help to dispel discouragement in our children by having them focus their thoughts on past successes and achievements. Children and adults alike become discouraged by their mistakes or poor performance. The Lord knew this discouragement would come, and he offered much encouragement to help us past these difficult moments.

Because of his past sins, the Apostle Paul must have suffered discouragement. He said, "I am the least of the apostles, . . . because I persecuted the church of God. But by the grace of God I am what I am; . . . but I laboured more abundantly than they all." (1 Corinthians 15:10.) Calling to his mind his fervent effort in spreading the word of Christ gave Paul courage, and he went on to give great instruction.

If we as parents can follow this example; then when a child slips into transgression we can dispel any thoughts of worthlessness and inability he may have by recalling to his mind past diligence and effort.

If a child comes home from school discouraged from a frustrating day, we must first strive to understand how he feels and to communicate this understanding. We can ask him about his past successes and let him tell us about them. If we talk long enough, he may come to see more vividly his accomplishments, and the present failure will not loom so large.

Sometimes we have a tendency to remember and to dwell on only the negative things we do. We need to recognize our mistakes so we can correct our course of action, but to unduly brood over them brings depression and negates progress. For example, Tim was making an airplane for a class display and became discouraged with it and wanted to quit. It is true that he bent the wing and it came off the plane, but the body part was really well done, and he could make another wing. Mother said, "Tim, you've done an excellent job on the fuselage. I'm sure if you try again on the wing you'll do better." When he did, he met with success.

Children can be taught to turn to something else for a time when they get discouraged with a particular project. Doing something—anything—constructive can lead them out of frustration.

Every child has creative energy that could and should be expressed in some worthwhile project. Directing his creative energies will accomplish much and will move him away from negative feelings. We derive great satisfaction from producing something original: drawing a picture, making up a song, sewing an article of clothing, making a model car, or working on a rock or doll collection.

Some children have hobbies they enjoy very much. Turning to these activities can help revitalize them and give them incentive and greater zest for tackling the difficult job again.

2. *Give assistance.*

We can help our children overcome discouragement by providing assistance when they get bogged down and discouraged with a particular job. Perhaps the job has taken longer than anticipated, or requires more skill than the child has, or is too complex and difficult for him to understand. Whatever the reason, there are times when a little assistance from a parent will get the child over the hump and give him encouragement to continue.

To give the right assistance at the right moment, parents need to be alert to signals of frustration and tension. Then we can move in before the discouragement takes over and makes it difficult to get the child back at the job. This also requires unselfishness on the part of the parents, the ability and willingness to put the child's needs first.

Suppose that as a child is working on his homework, we hear him grumble about "these dumb math problems." His discouragement may be felt as he restlessly shifts in his chair several times. We may read these signs and go over and say, "How's it coming?" or "That looks interesting. How do you do that problem?" or "Are the other problems like that?" Whatever we say should be aimed at showing interest and allowing the child to tell us what he's working on. This can lead to his saying that he doesn't understand a certain question, opening the door to the opportunity to give him the help he may need. With some children this may work better than saying, "Do you need some help?" Such a child may reply no when actually he would like help but feels embarrassed to admit it.

There are also times when children let fear of the unknown, such as new experience or a new task, foster discouragement. Planning in advance each step of the experience or task will help them conquer their fears and overcome discouragement.

Michael's Spanish class is planning a trip to Mexico at the end of the school year. Michael wants to go, but he is discouraged at the thought of earning the money to pay for the trip. His parents might encourage him by giving him a little extra money for his savings account to get him started. Then they could plan with him where he might go to look for work and ways to schedule his time so he could work enough hours to earn the needed amount. Such advance planning can go a long way to help the child overcome that discouraged, "I can't do it" feeling.

A parent's concerned and giving attitude can help the
child fight discouragement and let him know that he
doesn't have to tackle his problem alone.

3. *Show physical affection.*

Physical affection can reassure our children of our
loving concern and may help them feel confident to try
again. Such affection is comforting and reassuring.
When a child is discouraged, a little affection given at an
opportune moment can reassure him that we care for
him. What comforting assurance and courage the Prodi-
gal Son must have felt when he returned to his father:
"But when he was yet a great way off, his father saw him,
and had compassion, and ran, and fell on his neck, and
kissed him." (Luke 15:20.) That kind of love will give a
child courage to try again.

Feelings of inadequacy tend to draw us away from
others. Expressions of love are always encouraging,
though others may not respond to them at the moment.
A person needs time to absorb and remarshal his forces
before attacking problems again. "A time to embrace"
(Ecclesiastes 3:5) is the time when a child is hurt physically or emotionally. Physical affection can refill the res-
ervoir of courage he needs to meet life's challenges.

Janey had been dating Tim for almost four months
when suddenly he stopped calling. Two weeks later she
saw him with another girl. Dad's loving arm around her
as they sat together at church, and his genuine compliment about his pretty daughter, helped her fight feelings
of discouragement about herself.

Touch can sometimes communicate much better
than words, and we should use it to encourage our children and all our loved ones.

4. *Provide adequate rest and recreation.*

Rest and recreation can revive the spirit and check
discouragement; it is vital in order to maintain an attitude of vigor and courage. We are commanded to rest

on the Sabbath not only to keep the day holy, but also to "be refreshed." (Exodus 23:13.)

Children can learn to observe laws of good health by the example of their parents and through being taught to understand and rest their own bodies. Infants and young children are new in their bodies and have not yet learned how to properly control or understand their physical beings. Some parents let the child dictate when he will retire even though he is grouchy and teary the next day.

A little boy came to nursery school droopy-eyed and listless one day. He was almost too tired to talk, but he did manage to say, when I asked about what he did the night before, "I got too tired." His mother had told me that his cousins were visiting. This little fellow, wise for his years, could do nothing but sit and stare most of the morning.

Children naturally want to stay up late because they don't want to miss anything. They do not realize how quickly they tire; they get caught up in the excitement of activity and become exhausted if left to themselves.

Just as adults sometimes become so exhausted that they have difficulty sleeping, so also do children. They should be taught in their youth to sense when they are tired and then to rest themselves. We help them learn this by saying as we put them to bed, "My, doesn't it feel good to lie down," or, "It feels so good to rest." When they wake up, we can talk about how nice it feels to be rested and to feel the "invigorated mind and body." (See D&C 88:124.)

Other important aspects of good health that influence our attitudes are exercise and recreation. President Ezra Taft Benson has said: "Rest and physical exercise are essential, and a walk in the fresh air can refresh the spirit. Wholesome recreation is part of our religion, and a change of pace is necessary, and even its anticipation can lift the spirit." (*Ensign,* November 1974, p. 66.)

We all recognize the need for some recreation in our lives. President Brigham Young was especially diligent in encouraging good recreation for the Saints as they settled in the West, and he admonished the priesthood leaders to provide for the same. He was a great advocate of the importance of maintaining good health in order to do good work and further the progress of Zion. He said, "Let us seek to extend the present life to the uttermost, by observing every law of health, and by properly balancing labor, study, rest, and recreation, and thus prepare for a better life. Let us teach these principles to our children, that, in the morning of their days, they may be taught to lay the foundation of health and strength and constitution and power of life in their bodies." (*Discourses of Brigham Young*, p. 186.)

When our children get discouraged, they can be revived by engaging in some wholesome physical activity and recreation and then resting. Wholesome sports, dancing, plays, musicals, or movies can be good sources of recreation for our children to help them avoid discouragement and depression.

5. *Encourage service to others.*

Our children's discouragement can be dispelled as they serve others. Service to others is a basic principle of the gospel that we have been commanded to teach to our children: "Teach them to love one another, and to serve one another." (Mosiah 4:15.) Jesus taught that to serve others was to serve him: "Inasmuch as ye have done it unto one of the least of these my brethren, ye have done it unto me." (Matthew 25:40.) As King Benjamin pointed out, "When ye are in the service of your fellow beings ye are only in the service of your God." (Mosiah 2:17.)

Children particularly need guidance in giving service to those who are less fortunate. Their reaction to someone who is different is often rejection and disdain, but they can be taught compassion.

Jimmy, who was blind, was the object of curiosity

when he first came to nursery school. But gradually the children learned to have sympathy and love for him. One day he sat on the rug, rocking back and forth as he listened to some music, Julie went to the nearby fountain and got herself a drink. When she finished drinking, she noticed Jimmy. She looked at him and then at the fountain. Then she found a glass and filled it up. She glanced at Jimmy again and poured a little water out. She studied him again, trying to decide how much he would drink, then poured a little more from the glass. As she went over to Jimmy and carefully placed his hands around the glass, she said, "I brought you a drink, Jimmy." She waited as he drank it all, then took the glass back to the fountain. Beaming, she came over and tugged at my sleeve and said, "Teacher, I helped him."

Service is the greatest joy in the gospel. Children should be taught to understand that such joy can replace discouragement and depression if they turn their thoughts and deeds to loving and humble service to others.

6. *Cultivate friendships.*

To help them overcome discouragement, we should encourage our children to seek the company of true friends. Alma gives us an example of the love of two friends: "Now behold, this Lehi was a man who had been with Moroni in the more part of all his battles; and he was a man like unto Moroni, and they rejoiced in each other's safety; yea, they were beloved by each other." (Alma 53:2.)

David and Jonathan were another pair of great friends who helped each other in their trials, for "the soul of Jonathan was knit with the soul of David, and Jonathan loved him as his own soul." (1 Samuel 18:1.)

Some children have such charm that they develop friendships easily, but others must learn that "a man that hath friends must shew himself friendly." (Proverbs 18:24.) Wise parents can create circumstances, if necessary, to help their children develop good friendships. A child whose home is open and inviting to others can associate in a comfortable atmosphere where he can be more relaxed and therefore more friendly.

As children begin to move out into the neighborhood and enter school, friends play a vital role in their lives. Every child needs a friend to do things with. Acceptance by peers becomes increasingly important and reaches its peak as a child enters the teen years.

A child who is discouraged and not doing well in the classroom may feel buoyed up to try harder by the cheers of his friends at his physical powers on the playing ground. Fifteen-year-old Layne came home from school obviously feeling down about something. When his mother asked, "How did school go today?" he shrugged and said, "Okay, I guess." With a little prodding he confessed "I was a real klutz in P.E. today. Everything I did was wrong. Besides making some very dumb mistakes, I got yelled at by the coach for not being alert and watching better."

Later in the evening Layne's friends called and wanted to meet at the church to play basketball. He went with some reluctance, but came home cheerful and said to his mother, "Look at this." He took her out and showed her how he could now touch the rim of the basket. Layne's friends had cheered and encouraged him to try harder, and that made his efforts more successful.

Friends are a valuable asset and can provide strength particularly when difficulties arise. When Joseph Smith was in prison and feeling alone and forgotten, his words showed his great discouragement: "O God, where art thou? And where is the pavilion that covereth thy hiding place? How long shall thy hand be stayed?" As he continued to petition the Lord for assistance, these words of comfort were given: "Thy friends do stand by thee, and they shall hail thee again with warm hearts and friendly hands." (D&C 121:1-9.) Having "a friend that sticketh closer than a brother" (Proverbs 18: 24) can strengthen a child in many circumstances, and such friendships should be nurtured by parents.

7. *Read good books.*

Reading uplifting literature can help change a child's thoughts from depression to hope and courage. We have been counseled to "study and learn, and become acquainted with all good books." (D&C 90:15.) Children can enjoy many books that are fun to read and tell true stories of good people. The *Friend* magazine can be a handy source of uplifting material for parents to read to a despondent child. Emotions can be changed from hopelessness to courage through the use of books and magazines. Acquiring a collection of useful books to distract a child away from negative feelings may be well worth the effort and investment.

Nancy was feeling hurt and lonely because her peers had singled her out as the object of jokes and teasing. The teasing made her feel very self-conscious, depressed, and negative about herself. Sensing that something must be done to change the peer reaction, her mother said to Nancy, "Why don't you ask some of your friends over for a slumber party? You can all help me make pizza and caramel corn, and then I have a fun story to read out loud to you as you snuggle in your sleeping bags in the family room."

After careful planning, the invitations were sent out. The pizza and caramel corn were messy, but they provided good interaction between the girls. As the giggles subsided, Nancy's mother began to read *Ramona the Pest*. Soon the hilarious adventures of Ramona had the girls laughing together. As the story ended, Nancy's mother said, "I hope you girls can always have fun together and be kind to each other." As a result of the party, Nancy began to feel less sensitive to teasing, and the other girls became more accepting of her. They also began asking, "When can we have another party?"

Reading books about travel and adventure can give
the child an appreciation of other people and places as he
mentally visits new lands. Some children find mysteries
and science fiction very enjoyable in helping them to
relax and forget their problems for a time. Reading can
take the child's mind off his present troubles, which may
allow him to think more clearly when he faces the problem again.

Reading for pure pleasure—not for study or out of
necessity, but to have an experience that comes only
from the written page—can revive a child's courage.
When he is feeling discouraged, a parent might read to
him good books that he couldn't read himself, and thus
help him on to better feelings.

8. *Listen to uplifting music.*

Parents can teach their children to listen to uplifting
music to dissipate feelings of depression and discouragement. The Apostle Paul wrote: "Let the word of Christ
dwell in you richly in all wisdom; teaching and ad-
monishing one another in psalms and hymns and
spiritual songs, singing with grace in your hearts to the
Lord." (Colossians 3:16.)

Music has the ability to change our emotions and to
increase the depth of what we feel. When depression de-
scends, music can uplift and inspire us or it can deepen
the depression. The end result depends on the music we
choose.

"Music," said William Gladstone, "is one of the most
forceful instruments for governing the mind and spirit
of man." Elder Boyd K. Packer advises, "Our people
ought to be surrounded by good music of all kinds. Parents ought to foster good music in the home and cultivate
a desire to have their children learn the hymns of inspiration." (*Ensign,* January 1974, p. 27.)

Children love music and respond readily to it. Teenagers sometimes seek music as a bond with their friends.

Good men of all times have used music to enrich their

lives and to strengthen themselves. Saul, when he was troubled by an evil spirit, asked David to play for him on his harp. "David took an harp, and played with his hand: so Saul was refreshed, and was well, and the evil spirit departed from him." (1 Samuel 16:23.)

Paul admonished the Ephesians to speak among themselves "in psalms and hymns and spiritual songs, singing and making melody in your heart to the Lord." (Ephesians 5:19.) During his ministry on the earth, the Lord used music to prepare himself for his greatest test: "And when they had sung an hymn, they went out into the mount of Olives." (Mark 14:26.) We should teach our children to follow the example of our Savior in using inspired music to strengthen their lives.

9. *Introduce humor.*

Parents can teach their children to retain a sense of humor when difficulties arise. "A merry heart doeth good like a medicine," we read in Proverbs 17:22.

We all know that a little good humor will go a long way to see us through difficult circumstances. Each of our prophets, from Joseph Smith to Spencer W. Kimball, has displayed a sense of humor that has endeared him to people. Joseph Fielding Smith was viewed by some as quite an austere man, but he had a delightful sense of humor. When he was told that a certain man said he liked listening to all the Church leaders except Joseph Fielding Smith, because "He scares the hell out of me," President Smith clapped his hands in delight and responded, "That is exactly what I want to do, scare the hell out of him, then he'll be fit for a better place!" (*The Life of Joseph Fielding Smith,* p. 8.)

The Lord did not intend for us to go around with long, sober faces. If we follow the example of our leaders, we will help our children develop a sense of humor so that as trials come they will be able to "submit cheerfully and with patience to all the will of the Lord." (Mosiah 24:15.)

Most children become depressed about their appearance as they go through growth stages. Often they are
teased by friends. When my friends continued to tease
me about my height, I'd joke for a while and then turn to
one and say, "Why don't we laugh about your big nose
for a while. Ha ha." She didn't really have a big nose, but
it did change the focus of the teasing toward something
else.

Most of us do foolish and funny things occasionally,
and the ability to see the humor in our mistakes can keep
us from getting depressed and ease the embarrassment.

One day in class at the university, my students started
to chuckle and giggle whenever I turned around and
raised my arm to write on the board. I couldn't figure out
why they were laughing, so I just continued on as always.
After class I went to the nursery school to prepare some
materials for the children. As I reached for a bowl in the
cupboard, my student teacher burst out laughing and
then told me what was so funny. Apparently while I had
been dressing that morning, the label from my panty-
hose had come loose and was caught under my nylon
right behind my knee. Whenever I raised my arm, my
hem went up just enough to expose the label, which read
"Extra Long."

If we can teach the principle of humor, our children
will have that "merry heart" which "maketh a cheerful
countenance." (Proverbs 15:13.)

10. *Teach positive prayer.*

We need to teach our children that through prayer,
they can resist depressing influences and discouragement. In the Doctrine and Covenants we are told, "If
thou art sorrowful, call on the Lord thy God with suppli-
cation, that your souls may be joyful." (D&C 136:29.)

Children can learn while very young to go to their
Heavenly Father when they are discouraged or hurt.
Through prayer they can gain a real sense of the Father's
presence and comforting spirit. Children as young as

three or four can give beautiful prayers and can know and feel directly the Lord's tender concern for them.

At three-and-a-half, Rusty was an anxious little boy with many fears. He often became frightened at the thought of his mother leaving him or of getting lost when shopping or on other errands. His anxiety, combined with his temper when he couldn't have his own way, created difficulties for him when he played with others.

When the family went on a camping trip, Rusty was on the verge of crying as his father started them on a hike through the woods. As they walked deeper into the trees Rusty burst into tears at the thought of getting lost. His mother took him aside and said, "Let's have a prayer and ask Heavenly Father to watch over us and bring us back safe." Rusty was happy to say the prayer, and when they got back to camp he said, "Heavenly Father brought us back safe, huh, Mom!"

Later in the day, Rusty was fighting with his sister. Tired and upset, he said through his tears, "Mom, I'm having a bad day. Let's have a little prayer and then I'll be better." His mother took him to the tent where they could have privacy, and after the prayer she stayed close to see that no more fighting occurred. As Rusty snuggled down in his sleeping bag that night he said, "I was better, wasn't I, Mom. Jesus helped me and I didn't fight anymore."

Rusty had learned that his prayer for personal help was answered, and with further teaching and experience he could feel that Jesus would always be near to help him when he was upset and troubled or afraid.

Prayer is an essential part of the gospel. The scriptures contain many beautiful prayers. They are also full of admonitions concerning prayer, including one that is particularly applicable here: "And they shall . . . teach their children to pray, and to walk uprightly before the Lord." (D&C 68:28.) Through prayer children can learn that Jesus is a real person. They also learn that Satan is real, and that he desires to discourage them and wants them to fail, just as Jesus wants to help and protect them.

As a young adolescent I enjoyed the stories my grandmother told me about Germany. Her stories of the evil spirits that her family and others encountered commonly in her hometown of Ravensburg, Germany, made me shiver but were fascinating. One Sunday when we were visiting Grandma, she said to me, "The other day as I was going about my cooking and cleaning I felt so depressed and felt like the devil was standing right behind me. So I took my broom and made a swish behind my back and said, 'Get out of here, devil, and leave me alone.'" Grandma continued, "The evil spirit left me right then and there, and the rest of my day was pleasant."

Some of us don't realize how real that evil influence is. There may be times when our discouragement is caused not by wrongdoing in our lives but by the influence of the evil one. We have been told that we should call on the Lord at all times and that we should pray for strength to resist evil. The Lord himself prayed, "Deliver us from evil." (Matthew 6:13.)

When children experience unexplained or seemingly unfounded discouragement, they will be stronger for having been taught to turn to prayer. Prayer and faith in the Lord are essential tools they can use in overcoming discouragement.

Chapter 5

Provide Discipline and Punishment

My son, despise not the chastening of the Lord;
neither be weary of his correction:
for whom the Lord loveth he correcteth;
even as a father the son in whom he delighteth.
(Proverbs 3:11-12)

The word *discipline* comes from the word *disciple*, and means teaching or instructing. Instruction involves correction or chastening. The Lord chastens us to teach us obedience to his commandments. This chastening is necessary for positive growth. We read in Proverbs, "a child left to himself bringeth his mother shame." The passage goes on to explain how to remedy that situation: "Correct thy son, and he shall give thee rest." (Proverbs 29:15, 17.) Thus discipline, or correction, is aimed at strengthening or molding the child's character.

What does it mean to you to be punished? Many people responding to this question admit very negative feelings regarding punishment. They remember being angry, becoming resentful and hostile, and wanting revenge. They recall hurt, discouragement, and loss of self-esteem. Punishment unjustly or harshly given can and does bring such feelings, but can punishment still be an appropriate technique in guiding and teaching our children? Can it be used righteously? The obvious answer is yes.

The scriptures contain many illustrations of the Lord's punishment. (See, for example, Numbers 21:5-6; 2 Samuel 12:9-12; Mark 3:29; John 8:21; 1 Nephi 16:25; Mosiah 12:4-7; Alma 37:42; D&C 104:8; 105:6.) The second Article of Faith says, "We believe that men will be punished for their own sins."

To discipline and punish effectively in order to achieve positive results, we can look to the scriptures to see how the Lord uses punishment and what principles he applies in doing so.

In the scriptures the Lord uses the term *chasten* interchangeably with *punish*. The dictionary definition of *chasten* is to correct by punishment, to purify, to refine. Because we all sin, it is necessary to our progression that we be chastened or corrected so that we might repent. Punishment thus becomes a vital part of guiding our children to perfection. The scriptures verify this: "For all those who will not endure chastening, but deny me, cannot be sanctified." (D&C 101:5.)

Punishment involves imposing a penalty. None of us likes to be punished. Negative feelings are to be expected, as we see in these scriptures: "Chasten thy son while there is hope, and let not thy soul spare for his crying." (Proverbs 19:18.) "Now no chastening for the present seemeth to be joyous, but grievous: nevertheless afterward it yieldeth the peaceable fruit of righteousness unto them which are exercised thereby." (Hebrews 12:11.)

Punishment is indeed grievous to be borne, but if we practice the principles the Lord has given us, we can achieve "the peaceable fruit of righteousness" with our children.

Parents are constantly challenged to decide what actions are most beneficial in guiding their children. When a child misbehaves, first the parent encourages, redirects, or uses incentives or other means to move the child in the right direction. When these approaches are ineffective, discipline or punishment may be necessary.

Although there are several acceptable ways for disciplining or punishing a child, some methods are more effective than others. One method may be appropriate for one child but not for another. The same method may be beneficial and positive in one situation and detrimental in another. Parents should use their understanding of each child to make a wise decision as to which punishment would be best under the circumstances. The principal types of discipline or punishment fall into five categories: expressing disapproval, depriving the offender, isolating the wrongdoer, providing natural or logical consequences, and inflicting physical pain.

Expressing Disapproval

A misbehaving child must know that we disapprove of his inapproprioate behavior. To help the child recognize his mistakes, we should simply tell him what he is doing wrong, and, so he can understand, also explain why it is wrong. We may sometimes assume that the child knows better, and many times he does. But on most occasions we can state briefly what he should be doing and then act appropriately to see that he does it.

A verbal reprimand can be a very strong punishment. One scriptural example concerns the brother of Jared and his people who had pitched their tents by the seashore: "And it came to pass at the end of four years that the Lord came again unto the brother of Jared, and stood in a cloud and talked with him. And for the space of three hours did the Lord talk with the brother of Jared, and chastened him because he remembered not to call upon the name of the Lord." (Ether 2:14.)

A parent's tone of voice, facial expression, and body posture all communicate to the child the seriousness of his actions. Disapproval is really a part of all discipline and punishment.

Several negative ways in which parents occasionally show disapproval will bring negative results. Those that we should *not* use include the following: shaming the child, embarrassing him publicly, using sarcasm, assuming a martyr attitude, using profanity, screaming and yelling, refusing to speak to the child, and belittling.

Depriving the Offender

We should teach our children the eternal principle that some actions bring freedom and others bring restriction. Deprivation involves situations in which the parent denies the child special pleasures, favorite activities, or desired privileges. It may also include taking some cherished possession away from the child.

We as parents have the right and the responsibility to help our children exhibit their best behavior. In 1 Samuel we read about the family of Eli the prophet. The Lord, speaking to the child Samuel, said, "For I have told him [Eli] that I will judge his house for ever for the iniquity which he knoweth; because his sons made themselves vile, and he restrained them not." (1 Samuel 3:13.) Whenever a child's goals or activities conflict with those around him to the point that they infringe on the rights of others, the parents have a duty to restrain the child and redirect his activities.

Suggesting a more appropriate activity may be all that is required. If redirection and encouragement do not work, then parents need to take more forceful action. For example, if a child, after being warned, continues to use a toy in a way that is dangerous to others near him, it is legitimate to deprive him of the use of that particular toy and to stop the objectional behavior.

Isolating the Wrongdoer

Although isolation may be considered a form of deprivation, its effectiveness warrants a separate discussion. One of the strongest human desires is to belong to and be part of a family unit. Because the need for companionship is so basic to human nature, isolating a child is an effective means of punishment.

A major part of our eternal punishment or reward for our behavior on this earth concerns our association with others. Jesus said: "In my Father's house are many mansions: if it were not so, I would have told you. I go to prepare a place for you that where I am ye may be also." (John 14:2-3.) The use of isolation as a punishment may convince our children that they must live in a particular way if they are to enjoy the company of those whom they love.

The duration of the isolation should be determined by the child's change in attitude. The parent stipulates that he may rejoin the family when he is ready to change his behavior. It may take him only a few minutes to change his attitude and behavior—or it may take an hour. For the isolation to be effective, parents should follow through to see that the behavior is truly improved.

For example, a family was having company for dinner. Their oldest son, a five-year-old, was very excited and wanted to show off. As they were eating, the boy's behavior grew sillier and sillier. His father warned him to settle down, but he only got louder. After telling the boy twice to quiet down, the father got up quickly, removed the boy from the table, and took him to the next room. The guests heard some crying, and a moment later the father returned to the table. In a few minutes the boy came in, still wiping tears from his eyes, and sat down at the table, looking rather dejected. His mother later drew him into the conversation, and his father allowed him to help serve the ice cream.

Some children find it difficult to know what behavior is acceptable in different circumstances. We can tell our child what behavior is appropriate, but if we do not follow the words with action, he may assume that the way he is acting is acceptable. Clear explanation and thoughtful action will reinforce appropriate behavior.

Providing Natural or Logical Consequences

The scriptures are explicit in indicating that for every act there is a consequence, pleasant or unpleasant. Rewards are promised to those who faithfully live God's laws; punishment is decreed for the rebellious. (See Hosea 4:9; 2 Corinthians 9:6; Galatians 6:7.) Our choices in life will bring certain results. Children should learn that their behavior brings to bear other events in their lives. If they are made to feel and experience the natural or logical consequences of their behavior, they will be more knowledgeable in making wise decisions.

On many occasions the natural chain of events will bring a child all the punishment he needs. Self-inflicted guilt or anguish for wrongdoing is sometimes enough. In such a case the parents should not intervene: rather they should allow the child to suffer the aftermath of his actions. The teenager who gets up too late to catch the bus for school must walk. Clothes left on the floor instead of placed in the clothes hamper go unwashed.

Sometimes natural results are so far removed that the child has difficulty in seeing the repercussions of his deeds. It is then appropriate for the parent to use logical consequences.

Logical consequences involve situations wherein the parent structures events that might legitimately follow a misdeed. Using arranged effects requires good thinking and imagination in order to bring the outcome closer to the violation, thus aiding the child's understanding of cause and effect.

Each child in one family was required to come home directly after school before going to a friend's house to play. Salena often violated the rule. One afternoon her mother took the other children in the family to the dairy for ice cream. When Salena came home to find the others with ice cream cones, she asked, "Where is mine?" Her mother said, matter of factly, "I'm sorry you were not home in time to go with us."

The logical consequence of Salena's behavior was missing out on the treat. The mother did not gloat and say,"I told you so," or, "It serves you right." Rather she remained cheerful but sympathetic that the child had to learn obedience by missing the treat.·

Natural or logical consequences have limits and cannot be used in every situation. There are times when we as parents or teachers would be merciless to let our children feel the full weight of their transgressions. The natural consequence of playing in the street could be to be hit by a car; of course, we do not want our children to suffer to that extent. When our children are unwise, we sometimes need to be the protectors.

The Savior does not let us suffer the full weight of our sins if we repent and believe in him. He has said, "Therefore I command you to repent—repent, lest I smite you by the rod of my mouth, and by my wrath, and by my anger, and your sufferings be sore—how sore you know not, how exquisite you know not, yea, how hard to bear you know not. For behold, I, God, have suffered these things for all, that they might not suffer if they would repent." (D&C 19:15-16.)

The eternal truth is that we will reap the punishments or rewards of our acts. The Lord has told us: "There is a law, irrevocably decreed in heaven before the foundations of this world, upon which all blessings are predicated—and when we obtain any blessing from God, it is by obedience to that law upon which it is predicated." (D&C 130:20-21.) We want our children to understand this eternal principle.

Inflicting Physical Pain

Inflicting physical pain is the technique most people mention when asked about punishment. In frustration, many parents resort to slapping, spanking, or hitting the child when nothing else seems to work. Sometimes when we punish our children we are not thinking of their best interest, but seem bent only on venting our own anger.

Like almost everything in this world, physical punishment can be misused and distorted; it can be harmful and even evil and unrighteous. Sometimes parents have seen so often the misuses and the damage it does that they are afraid to use it at all.

Elder Bruce R. McConkie has stated that the chastening of the Lord may take "the form of chastisement, meaning corporal punishment." (*Mormon Doctrine,* p. 122.) "He that will not bear chastisement is not worthy of my kingdom," the Lord has said. (D&C 136:31.) Isaiah prophesied of the Lord's wounds of chastisement that He would bear for our sakes: "But he was wounded for our transgressions, he was bruised for our iniquities: the chastisement of our peace was upon him; and with his stripes we are healed." (Isaiah 53:5.)

We read in the Book of Mormon that "except the Lord doth chasten his people with many afflictions, yea, except he doth visit them with death and with terror, and with famine and with all manner of pestilence, they will not remember him." (Helaman 12:3.)

Inflicting physical pain on a child can be an appropriate punishment. This may sound harsh, but spanking can have a place in good guidance. There are times when a quick, sharp slap on the rear end of an unruly child can be a good method of correction. With some children in some circumstances, spanking may be the best solution. Knowing when and to what degree to use physical pain as punishment should be a matter of prayerful consideration. If we apply scriptural principles, we can learn to use spanking sparingly and righteously.

Principles of Discipline and Chastisement

One basic scriptural concept that we must always keep in mind as we deal with our children is this: "No power or influence can or ought to be maintained . . . only by persuasion, by long-suffering, by gentleness or meekness, or by love unfeigned; by kindness, and pure knowledge, which shall greatly enlarge the soul without hypocrisy, and without guile." (D&C 121:41-42.) With this concept as a guide, let us examine some principles of effective discipline.

1. *Exercise emotional control.*

As parents exercise control over their emotions, they will see more clearly and judge more wisely when punishment becomes necessary. In the Bible we read: "He that is slow to wrath is of great understanding: but he that is hasty of spirit exalteth folly." (Proverbs 14:29.)

When a person is emotionally upset—angry, embarrassed, or jealous—he seldom exercises good judgment. Punishment given in uncontrolled anger is generally too harsh and causes fear and resentment that damage the parent's relationship with his child.

Julie was on the stand participating in the Easter presentation with her Primary class. As the children sang, Jan, the child next to Julie, gave Julie a push. Julie pushed back. Jan then pinched her, and Julie pinched her back and pushed her away. The two girls pinched and pushed each other through the entire song. By the time the number was over, Julie's father was red in the face at her behavior. He quickly grabbed her, took her out, spanked her very hard, and then ordered her not to cry. Julie cried, and her father threatened more spanking if she made any further whimpers. Julie held the tears in until she got home. Then she ran to her room and screamed and screamed at the top of her lungs.

The father was so embarrassed at his child's behavior that he could not see the situation from Julie's standpoint. If he had controlled his emotions, he could have seen what a difficult situation it was for Julie and could have said, "Next time someone pushes you, ignore them; and if they continue, then just move out of reach."

Emotional control is essential when punishment is

necessary. Note that the scriptures don't say "Do not get
angry," but rather, be "slow to wrath." (Proverbs 14:29.)
It will help the child if, when we give a warning, we also
state that we are becoming angry, and that if he doesn't
stop, we will become very angry.

Some feel that parents should not punish in anger at
all. If a parent cannot control his anger, then he definitely should not punish in anger. But there are times
when parents should get angry—their children need to
know how to control and express anger properly.

2. *Give fair warning.*

Before parents impose a penalty, they should warn
their children specifically what penalty would be forth-
coming if they continue misbehaving.

Most of us will agree that it is unfair to impose a stiff
penalty upon a child for misbehavior if he does not know
that such behavior will bring a penalty. The Lord in his
mercy does not bring the full punishment of the law
upon those who do not have the law given to them. In a
revelation given through the Prophet Joseph Smith, the
Lord said: "Behold, I sent you out to testify and warn the
people. . . . Therefore they are left without excuse, and
their sins are upon their own heads." (D&C 88:81-82.) As
this scripture and others indicate, the Lord does not
punish his people without first sending prophets to warn
them of impending destruction if they do not mend their
ways. Many times a knowledge of the penalty will be
forceful enough to motivate a person to make a change.
Alma says, "If there was no law given against sin men
would not be afraid to sin." (Alma 42:20.) This principle
works in many small ways to teach children the consequences of their actions.

A mother can keep a warning from becoming a threat
by making sure the children know she will do what she
says. She should not give a warning she does not intend
to enforce. For example, some friends stopped by to visit
one family. After greeting the guests, the children went

to the other end of the room to play. Soon their play became excessively loud. Their mother went over and told the children that they needed to play quietly or they would have to leave the room. The children quieted for a moment and then became very loud again. At that point the mother should have enforced what she had said. She should have told the children to leave the room and then seen that they did so.

Parents should provide their children with avenues of freedom and activity by telling them what they can do instead of what they can't do. They should also state things in a positive way. When a child starts to hit his sister, the parent's most immediate response will probably be: "Stop! No!" Then, after he stops the child, he can add, "You may pound on this pounding board." The child already knows he should not hit his sister; the parent's words provide an alternative action and give him some appropriate redirection. Then, if he still continues in his misbehavior, the parent can give the warning for not obeying, and follow through with discipline.

3. *Let the child know why he is being punished.*

Discipline and punishment are aimed at stopping undesirable behavior and changing it to something more acceptable. Parents certainly cannot achieve this goal if their children do not understand why they are being punished and what behavior they are supposed to change.

The nursery children were pasting pictures of autumn leaves. Jamie was quite exuberant with the glue and began teasing the other children by dabbing glue on their hands and clothes. I warned him, "The glue is to be used for gluing the leaves only. You must keep it on the paper." He continued his teasing.

I became annoyed, as I had had experience with the glue and knew it was very hard to clean up, so I said, "I will have to take the glue away from you if you do not use it properly."

Jamie settled down for a minute, then began again, this time getting a big glob of glue into Mike's hair. I got up quickly, grabbed him by the shoulders, and lifted him off the floor. Drawing his face close to mine, with my eyes wide, nose flared, and voice raised, I said, "I'm angry!" Still holding him by the shoulders, I carried him away from the group, set him down hard on a chair, and said, "Now you sit there until you decide you can use the glue without getting it on anything *but* the paper!"

Jamie's lips quivered and a tear dropped. Because his removal from the group was immediate, he had no doubt as to why he was not allowed to stay with them. He was still sitting apart when I returned from washing the glue from Mike's hair. After a few minutes he got up and took a step toward the table where the other children were working. I looked over at him and asked, "Are you ready to join the group now?" He nodded and I said, "Okay, come over." After he had pasted for a minute, I went over and put my arm around him and admired his picture. He smiled and was his happy self again.

An interesting side effect was that all the other children were especially careful with the glue the rest of the day.

When a child is unkind to a brother, sister, or friend, he should not be allowed to play with that person for a time. When he abuses a privilege, he should have the privilege withdrawn for a short while. When he destroys someone's things, he should have to replace them. When he is rude in the presence of family or friends, he should be denied their company for a while.

This type of discipline makes much more sense to the child than a spanking or some other unrelated action. "The commission of crime should be punished according to the nature of the offense." (D&C 134:8.)

In order to give our children a clear understanding of why certain behavior brings punishment, we can do as the scriptures suggest and reason together. The scriptures state that the Lord reasons with us so we may come to a clearer understanding of what he requires. (See Isaiah 1:18; D&C 45:9-10; 50:10-12.) We can do the same with our own children.

During this reasoning process, parents should state why a certain behavior is expected. The child will more readily agree with what the parent desires if he knows the reasonable explanation for the requirement. He will also be more inclined to be obedient when he understands the punishment for disobedience.

4. *Adapt the punishment to the individual.*

Parents should carefully consider each child's temperament and personality in choosing the appropriate form of punishment. Each of us is a unique individual. Not only do we look different from each other, but we all respond differently to our environment. Our perceptions are selective; as two look at a picture, each one sees meaning in different parts.

As we come to a time of disciplining, we should consider the individual. We cannot successfully apply the same punishment to every child. We cannot apply any principle shotgun-style. Each one must be used in view of individual responses. Isolation may be punishment to one child but reward to another.

Blaine, my older brother, once asked Mother if he could go to a party. She joked with him and teased, "Oh, you don't want to go there. It will probably be a dull party with all the duddy girls in town." He protested and said it sounded great. She continued to joke about what bad food and dumb games there would be. He still insisted he wanted to go.

As I listened to this exchange I thought, *Why doesn't she just come right out and tell him no?* But she didn't. She continued to joke. After a few minutes, he went to the phone and called his friend and said, "Mother says I can't go." I thought, *What? She never said that.*

Had I been in his place, I would have known that

Mother didn't want me to go, but I might have gone anyway. I asked her later, "Why didn't you just tell him no and save all the round-about-the-bush business?"

She explained, "Your brother is different from you. If I were to lay down the law as you suggest, he would rebel and defy me. Even as a child, your brother was always strong-willed; he responded much better when I joked and teased and cajoled him into obedience. I could never spank him as I did your younger brother. When I tried spanking, Blaine would just sit there with a belligerent, defiant, 'you-can-beat-me-purple-and-I-won't-do-it' look. So I never spanked him. I reprimanded with words only.

"Now, your younger brother is altogether different," she continued. "I can talk to him until I'm blue in the face, and he doesn't budge. But if I give him a spank, he is a much better boy and does what he should. He seems to need more action and less talk."

When different punishments are used, the children might complain when one gets spanked and the other doesn't. If we take the necessary time to explain these differences, the children will come to recognize the individuality of each person in the family and to be patient when those differences cause problems. The justice and the reasons behind our actions will teach them to remember these same considerations in teaching their own children.

5. *Require that the wrong be made right.*

When a child has transgressed, we should provide a way for him to improve his behavior or to make restitution. In the Doctrine and Covenants we are told: "Verily, thus saith the Lord unto you whom I love, . . . whom I love I chasten that their sins may be forgiven, for with the chastisement I prepare a way for their deliverance in all things out of temptation, and I have loved you." (D&C 95:1.) This scripture emphasizes the significance of expressing love when punishment is necessary. In fact, the Lord implies that punishment is an act of love.

Loving involves providing a way for the child to make restitution when he gets into a difficult situation. We should provide for him a graceful way out of the dilemma. Whenever possible, we should help him repair any damage he has done.

At nursery school, Darren was playing with the crepe-paper trim on the bulletin board. Though I told him to find something else to play with, he persisted and ended up tearing the crepe paper off. When I saw that he had ripped the display and torn some of the trim, I told him he could not go outside to play—that he was confined to indoors. Since outdoor play was his favorite activity, he stomped around the room and tugged at the door, which I blocked. He said, "I'm mad at you. I want to go out."

I replied, "I'm sorry, but you cannot. I warned you, but you tore the display anyway."

He continued to storm around the room, shouting, "I'm mad," and again tugged at the door.

I said, "I'm sorry, you can't go out—unless you want to fix the display and make it look like it did before. If you will fix it, you may go outside. I don't want a sloppy job. It must look pretty when you are finished."

Darren's face lit up. "Yeah, I'll fix it." He worked enthusiastically until he finished the repair. Afterward he was pleased with himself and felt good toward me.

The principle of requiring that the wrong be made right is particularly important when a parent is using deprivation as the punishment. There must be a clear-cut method for the child to earn back the privileges he has been deprived of.

6. *Show an increase of love.*

After parents have punished a child, they should reassure him by showing increased love. The Lord has admonished us: "[reprove] betimes with sharpness, when moved upon by the Holy Ghost; and then [show] forth afterwards an increase of love toward him whom thou hast reproved, lest he esteem us to be his enemy."

(D&C 121:43.) Children can and do get the mistaken idea that we don't love them anymore when we punish without applying this principle.

After a child has been punished he may say, "You don't love me. You're a mean Mommy." Then he may hide from his mother. In this situation she should show that she does care by extending that increase of love. After a little time she might seek out the child to do something pleasant with him. Or she might take the first opportunity to give the child special attention, extra love, or an unexpected privilege. This, as the scripture states, is necessary, "lest he esteem thee to be his enemy."

Punishing properly is truly loving a child to the point of taking action to help him live a better life, as shown in the following example:

Brad was always a fun-loving and often mischievous child. As he reached his teens, he grew to be more daring in participating in deviant activities, although he continued to be active in his ward's youth programs. When he entered high school his daring and choice of friends led him into more serious transgression. He didn't openly rebel against his family, but he was slowly drawn into Satan's whirlpool as he became involved in drugs and immorality. He left high school to marry and then joined the army. Army life took him farther from the gospel, and he became involved in even more sin.

Brad's father went through searching torment, questioning how he had failed. Had he been too severe in his discipline and punishment? Had he neglected to spend enough time with him? Communication had been open, but nothing had yet turned Brad from his path of self-destruction. His parents continued to reach out and tried never to condemn. When the early marriage came, they welcomed the young woman and tried to help the couple get a start; they also urged both to discontinue the use of drugs and alcohol.

Brad's discharge from the army brought only more

complications, and finally he left his wife and child and totally embraced a life of transgression in a distant state. When a bad experience with drugs left him almost incoherent, Brad called his father, who flew out immediately and drove him home to put him in the hospital. The father's heart wept to see his son so devastated by sin.

When Brad was discharged from the hospital, he decided to return to his wife, even though their life together had been stormy and uncertain. Throughout it all she had remained loyal and supportive. His father visited them as often as he could and offered to help when Brad would let him, but he was painfully aware that his only effective tool was his love for Brad.

Still on drugs and liquor, Brad was unable to hold a job. When his funds ran out, he would come to his father to borrow money. The father would always give him some money along with a box of food and an invitation to come by any time and take from the storeroom whatever he needed. He was also careful not to be critical of the long hair, beard, and grubby clothes. Rather, he continued to encourage Brad and try to draw him back into living the principles of the gospel.

Suffering from much inner torment, Brad finally decided to go to his bishop and confess. With much encouragement and assurance and a kind and gentle demeanor, the bishop was able to draw Brad into his office just as Brad was losing courage. Though Brad's confession helped him considerably, he still doubted his ability to live the gospel. But gradually, with blessings from his father and with much talk and prayer, he made slow steps toward returning to the Church.

At first Brad started paying some tithing. Attending church meetings was hard, because he felt uncomfortable. Bishops, home teachers, and neighbors reached out repeatedly. Years passed, and finally, little by little, Brad was able to give up tobacco, treat his wife and children more kindly, attend church more regularly, read the scriptures, and lead his family in prayer. During the long way back, his father said nothing about the beer cans in the car, nor about the unkempt children, nor many other little things it would have been easy to comment on.

At last, fully repentant and living the gospel, Brad received a patriarchal blessing. A few weeks later his wife received her blessing. These were landmark spiritual experiences for them. Now progress was almost unbelievably fast, until Brad's father wept with joy to see his son kneel at the temple altar with his wife and children around him.

Later, when his father asked him what had helped him most to come back into the gospel and full activity in the Church, Brad replied, "Dad, no matter what I did, or how bad it was, I always knew you loved me."

The methods and principles of punishment work in harmony, with increase of love being the governing one that should influence all the others. When we use scriptural principles in dealing with disobedience, our children will eventually see our punishing as an act of love and will learn that "the ear that heareth the reproof of life abideth among the wise," and "he that heareth reproof getteth understanding." (Proverbs 15:31-32.)

Chapter 6
Instill Responsibility

For it is required of the Lord,
at the hand of every steward,
to render an account of his stewardship,
both in time and in eternity.
(D&C 72:3)

The Lord has said, "A commandment I give unto you, that ye shall organize yourselves and appoint every man his stewardship." (D&C 104:11.) As children grow they should be given responsibility, so that at maturity they will be wise stewards, knowing how to conduct themselves properly and to be accountable for their conduct.

For our children to develop as responsible individuals, they need experience in decision making, knowledge of their duty, and freedom of choice. Samuel the Lamanite warned, "Behold, ye are free . . . to act for yourselves; for behold, God hath given unto you a knowledge and he hath made you free." (Helaman 14:30.) Careful and diligent effort is necessary to teach the child to be accountable. Starting with small, everyday tasks, a child can learn this important principle. The Lord has said that he would "make every man accountable, as a steward over earthly blessings." (D&C 104:13.)

Principles for Teaching Responsibility

1. *Start with small tasks.*

To foster responsible behavior in our children, we should assign small tasks at first and add greater responsibilities as they grow. Jesus' parable of the talents says that he who has been "faithful over a few things" will be made a "ruler over many things." (See Matthew 25:14-29.) Therefore, he tells us, "be not weary in well-doing, for ye are laying the foundation of a great work. And out of small things proceedeth that which is great." (D&C 64:33.)

Children need experience in being responsible. To teach accountability, we might ask ourselves, "At what age should I start, and what responsibilities can I give him to teach him this virtue?"

A favorite expression of my two-year-old daughter is "Me do that," as she insists on dressing, undressing, and washing herself. This is a prime time to teach responsibility and independence. Although she cannot yet tie her shoes, she may be able to put them on by herself. She may still need assistance, but she should be allowed to do as much as she can, even if the job takes longer and looks less than perfect.

One day Jimmy came to nursery school grinning widely. His hair looked as if he had used a whole bottle of hair cream to slick it down. He wore one green sock and one blue one. I said, "My, your hair looks so smooth." Still beaming with pride, he said, "Yes, I combed it myself." His mother, standing behind him, added rather sheepishly, "He wanted to get ready for school all by himself today."

Caring for his own personal needs and belongings and helping with household chores are tasks that give a child the base for further growth in accountability. Encouraging him in his attempts at these things when he is young will further such behavior when he is older. If a child is old enough to pick up a toy to play with, he is old enough to pick it up to put it away. The parent who works with the child will, to begin with, probably do most of the job, but as the child grows in coordination and understanding, he can assume more of the work himself. Children really do want to help; they feel a part of things and receive satisfaction when they contribute to the order of the home.

As one family completed plans for a camping and fishing trip, the father assigned Jim, age twelve, to get the wood for the campfire each day. Tommy, age ten, was to carry the water from the supply faucet whenever it was needed. As their mother began discussing the meals, Mark, age four, piped up with, "Hey, what do I get to do?" The father, thinking quickly, said, "Oh, I almost forgot. You are to check the worms for our fishing every day and dig for more so we don't run out."

Although the father had already planned for an ample worm supply, he sensed that Mark needed a job to make him feel important and a part of the family. Mark accepted this small job with pride and diligence.

When they got home, the parents laughed when they saw that, in spite of all the worms they had used, they had more than when they had started.

One mother was having trouble getting her four-year-old daughter, Sally, to put away her clothes and toys. Even when they worked together, Sally did as little as possible. To deal with this situation, her mother would say, "Sally, you will need to put your clothes away *before* lunch (or before you go outside)." When Sally headed for the door, her mother would say in a pleasant voice, "Oh, you forgot to put your toys away. You'll need to do so before you leave." Then she would enforce the assignment cheerfully. There was no need for her to nag; she would simply restate what Sally must do.

Consistency is important in following through on the performance of little daily tasks. Parents should not allow themselves to become so busy with other things that they forget to watch, and allow the child to slip out without completing the assigned task. Remember, being consistent is vital!

2. *Work together.*

Parents can teach skills and correct procedures more effectively if they work together with their children. Every individual in the family can make some contribution for the good of the whole. Remember Paul's words: "The eye cannot say unto the hand, I have no need of thee: nor again the head to the feet, I have no need of you." (1 Corinthians 12:21.)

If we remember this scripture in working with our children, we can help them feel that the contributions they make are worthwhile and can also find opportunities to instruct them. Working with our children, we can teach the skills they will need in order to learn the virtue of responsibility.

As one mother prepared the meat for the dinner, her daughter prepared the vegetable, and her son, the salad. This cooperative effort gave the mother a chance to direct their efforts and to give any needed assistance. Since she was working with them, the children were happy to help and took pride in doing their parts well.

Sometimes when parents assign a child to do a job without also giving him the proper guidance, the child may say to himself, "I'm the only one who has to work around here," or "Why do I always have to do everything?" Children will not be so likely to complain if their parents work with them on occasion.

A mother says to her son, "Go clean your room." When she checks later, she finds that it looks clean, but then she discovers that the toys have been shoved under the bed and the clothes have been tossed in the bottom of the closet. If she had said, "Let's go clean your room" and had worked with him until the standard of performance was clear and the expected behavior established, she would have been able to ask him to clean the room without giving further assistance.

＊Working together provides other benefits. The child's work can be more satisfying to him and he can develop more proficient skills if one of his parents works with him and gives on-the-spot praise and recognition. Parents should recognize the pleasure in working with their children, whether it is in cleaning the house, grooming the lawns and yard, weeding the garden, or cultivating the farm. Such times can be happy times of sharing and love and provide wonderful occasions for teaching responsibility.

3. *Teach diligence to duty*.

Once a child knows his responsibilities, he needs to be encouraged to be diligent in performing them. President David O. McKay said, "Two principles are inherent in individual responsibility: First, the learning, the knowing what one's duty is; second, to act in all diligence in performance of that duty." (*Secrets of a Happy Life,* p. 144.) A child learns his duty by observing examples and receiving specific instructions.

The Lord has provided written references that we should search to learn our duty: "Let every man learn his duty, and to act in the office in which he is appointed in all diligence." (D&C 107:99.) Past and modern prophets have given similar counsel.

Teaching children their responsibilities is not nearly as difficult as getting them to be diligent in doing them. Many of us—children and adults alike—start off with ambition and great fervor, but as the task continues and problems arise, we slack off and may even leave the job half finished.

The scriptures are replete with examples of individuals who started out well but did not continue as they commenced. David was a great king in Israel and was loved and honored of the Lord. His beginning was marked by earnest and righteous devotion, but he faltered along the way when he gave in to his desire for Bathsheba. (See 2 Samuel 11:1-27.)

Oliver Cowdery began his labors in the kingdom with faithful and humble service, and he was rewarded of the Lord with the gift to translate. But later, when he failed, the Lord said, "It is because that you did not continue as you commenced." (D&C 9:5.) Because Oliver had not continued in his righteous efforts, the gift was taken from him.

Elder Rex D. Pinegar has stated: "To continue means more than to endure or to tolerate something. It means to maintain a steady course of action with unshaken faith in Christ. It means to be a true follower of Christ." (*Ensign*, November 1974, p.44.) "Then said Jesus to those Jews which believed on him, If ye continue in my word, then are ye my disciples indeed." (John 8:31.)

Children will be motivated to greater diligence if they see our example and receive our encouragement to "press forward." As a father hurries off to priesthood meeting on a snowy, cold Sunday morning, his young son at home sees this clear example. As a mother works hard preparing a lovely meal for her family, her children see and learn from her example. They come to realize that the necessary duties in their family are performed by devoted, caring parents. Children who are neglected and left to themselves are the ones who show irresponsibility to family and community.

✶ A parent who works hard, even when tired, shows his children that there are times when one must work even though he feels like quitting. Some individuals feel that a little tiredness is a legitimate reason for stopping; they have not been taught to work until the job is done.

During my youth, we spent summers on our wheat farm in Montana. When the wheat was ready, we worked continuously into the night and sometimes until the dew fell. Those were long, hard hours, but there was great satisfaction in working together to harvest what we had labored over all year.

There were times, as we were doing the ordinary cleaning around the house, when I became tired and asked Mother, "Why don't we just leave it and finish it tomorrow?" She'd reply, "Each day brings its own work. We may want to do something else tomorrow or something else may come up and we wouldn't be able to get back to this, so we'd better finish it now." She'd let me rest for a few minutes and then urge me back to the job. Many times something else did come up, and procrastination would have left the job unfinished. "He that is slothful in his work is brother to him that is a great waster." (Proverbs 18:9.)

Latter-day Saints have been known as diligent, industrious people. We want to instill in our children a sense of responsibility, a love for work, and a desire to do it with excellence and pride. But since the advent of television, it seems that a generation of watchers instead of doers is developing. The emphasis on leisure time as the goal of the good life is a formidable enemy in teaching diligence and responsibility. The counsel of the Lord to Adam is as valid today as it was when it was given: "Cursed is the ground for thy sake; . . . thorns also and thistles shall it bring forth to thee; . . . In the sweat of thy face shalt thou eat bread." (Genesis 3:17-19.)

Children, if guided correctly, will learn for themselves the inner satisfaction of good effort and time well spent. The Lord has said, "Let . . . all the works which I have appointed unto you, be continued on and not cease; and let your diligence, and your perseverance, and patience, and your works be redoubled, and you shall in nowise lose your reward." (D&C 127:4.)

4. *Find the fun in work.*

Children will learn to love work as parents make jobs fun and enjoyable and as they encourage superior performance.

Young children, by nature, find satisfaction and enjoyment in doing necessary things such as washing hands, sweeping the floor, and taking a bath. Parents should capitalize on this natural pleasure. The parental attitude is all-important in developing within the child the attitude of love of work. A helpful suggestion given in the song "A Spoonful of Sugar" is to make every task "a lark, a spree." This can be true of most things. If parents can find the fun in a job, it can become a lark and a game to children.

Some time ago I was visiting my sister who was seven months pregnant. Unable to scrub the floor herself, she had assigned the task to Teresa, her nine-year-old daughter. As we sat in the living room visiting, Teresa kept grumbling from the kitchen, "I don't want to do this. This is hard." Finally I went to the kitchen and jokingly asked, "Why don't you tie the brush on your foot and skate around?" Teresa laughed and said, "Silly, that wouldn't work." "Okay, then put on your favorite record and skate with your hands. You have to get it done, so you might as well enjoy it. If you want me to, I'll stand over you and beat you with a wet noodle till you get it done." She laughed again. I left, and she finished quickly. As she came into the living room, I said, "My, you got that done in a hurry. See, scrubbing can be fun." She smiled and agreed, "Well, it wasn't too bad."

If we can't make something fun, at least we can make it tolerable or less painful. Music has a great ability to lift us beyond the mundane things of life. If we use music with our work, we can make it enjoyable.

The song "Whistle While You Work" describes how important music can be when it is used with work. Children should be encouraged to discipline themselves to do necessary things that are not too pleasant. Music can aid them in achieving this goal.

As all must work, a cheerful attitude toward what must be done will produce a happier life. "He that is of a merry heart hath a continual feast." (Proverbs

15:15.) Satisfaction and pleasure in a job well done are important attitudes for children to develop. Then perhaps, after a long, fruitful life, they can say as did Thomas Edison, "I never did a day's work in my life—it was all fun."

5. *Instruct in money management.*

Children learn to manage money more successfully if they receive guidance and direction from parents and have actual experience with money.

Nephi counseled, "Wherefore, do not spend for that which is of no worth, nor your labor for that which cannot satisfy." (2 Nephi 9:51.) This reiterates Isaiah's instruction: "Wherefore do ye spend money for that which is not bread? and your labour for that which satisfieth not?" (Isaiah 55:2.) Children need proper training to develop the skills necessary to become financially responsible adults.

A few guidelines may help parents in teaching their children to be wise and prudent in earning, planning for expenditures, saving regularly, and making wise use of credit.

(a) *Provide each child with money, according to a definite plan, that he is responsible to manage.* Ordinarily children obtain money in one of three ways: an allowance, earnings at home or away from home, or a dole when they request it. Giving money to a child on request has several disadvantages. Parents usually end up handing over much more than they realize, and as a by-product, the child may think there is an unlimited supply available only for the asking. The dole system does not provide proper training for advance planning, nor does it teach the importance of earning what one receives.

Children usually want to spend money long before they can be employed outside the home. An allowance coupled with the opportunity to earn money in the home will provide them with the experience that will teach the value of money in terms of time and effort.

(b) *Along with the allowance, provide guidance and train-*

ing in money management. As parents instruct their children on the law of tithing, the importance of saving, and the idea of using their money for worthwhile things, they will build a sound base from which to function as situations occur. If children learn to pay tithing and save from each allowance, "whether it be little or much" (D&C 63:40), they will likely continue these practices as they mature and their earnings increase.

(c) *Give children opportunities to share in family financial planning so that they can learn about their role in relation to that of the entire family.* Including children in some of the family planning for the use of money will give them necessary lessons in financial obligation. They should learn that housing, food, utilities, taxes, and health needs must all be paid for.

One father taught his children about money obligations in a family home evening. He gave each child an equal share of one-dollar bills from his previously cashed monthly paycheck. Then he laid before the family the bills to be paid that month. The house payment was to be paid first. Everyone put in an equal number of his or her dollars to cover that bill. Next came the utilities; each again put into the middle pile some of his or her dollars. And so it continued with each obligation. The children were astonished to see how much money it took for these necessary obligations and how little was left for fun and entertainment. They became less demanding, and the older ones were stimulated to try to earn money outside the home for the extra things they wanted.

6. *Inspire initiative.*

Parents can stimulate their children to use initiative in all their responsibilities and to perform with excellence more than is required.

The Lord has told us, "For behold, it is not meet that I should command in all things; for he that is compelled in all things, the same is a slothful and not a wise servant; wherefore he receiveth no reward. Verily I say, men should be anxiously engaged in a good cause, and do many things of their own free will, and bring to pass much righteousness; for the power is in them, wherein they are agents unto themselves." (D&C 58:26-28.) This scripture points out an important principle of responsibility: we should take the initiative and do much good of our own free will, and do what is asked and more. This is an extension of the doctrine of the second mile: "And whosoever shall compel thee to go a mile, go with him twain." (Matthew 5:41.)

The philosophy of the world advocates doing just what has to be done and no more. In many jobs, the goal of the worker is to do the bare minimum. The employee who does not follow that code may find himself mocked and jeered as a fool. Other workers may accuse him of "apple polishing," or feel he has ulterior motives.

Elder Franklin D. Richards has said, "The desire for superior achievement comes from our Father in heaven. However, many people are imbued with the spirit of 'just getting by.' This spirit comes from the evil one. Let us avoid the habit of 'just getting by,' as it will rob us of the choicest rewards. Whether our work is mainly mental or physical or is a combination of both, we should learn to do it well, cultivate the proper attitude, and develop work habits that will produce superior results." (*Improvement Era*, December 1969, p. 102.)

Children need to observe the example of their parents in learning to work for excellence and to show initiative. Initiative is a hard lesson to learn, for most of us like to know what's expected, then to do it and be done. But if we do only what is asked, we are considered by the Lord as slothful servants. Even though there will always be those who jeer at those who do extra, there will also be the employer who looks for the hard worker—the worker who gives a full day's labor for his wages, who is honest in his work and earns the pay he receives.

Along with the other faculty members, it was my responsibility at Brigham Young University to evaluate students after their experience in practice teaching. To make our evaluations more helpful, we met with the superintendents who hire new teachers in the public schools. They all stressed one item on the evaluation sheet: initiative. They said, "Initiative is the first item we look for. If the prospective teacher is marked below 'very good,' he is hardly given a second thought." These leaders indicated clearly that employers don't want anyone who has to be prodded to get things done. They look for someone who can see what needs to be done and then does it.

Latter-day Saints have been given great knowledge of the truth and have received much instruction as to their duty to the Lord. They are indeed without excuse, because they know what is expected, and that they will be held accountable for those things they should have done and did not. "Therefore to him that knoweth to do good, and doeth it not, to him it is sin," James said. (James 4:17.)

We will be held accountable for those good things we didn't do as well as for those wicked things we did do. Many are victims of the same weakness and feel to lament, as Paul did, "For the good that I would I do not: but the evil which I would not, that I do." (Romans 7:19.) Many sit back and do only that which is necessary; they do not exert themselves to excel and to find how they could make their own unique contribution.

As a child of nine or ten I wanted to live one day perfectly. My parents had diligently taught me the truths of the gospel, and I understood them as much as a child could and felt a desire to repent of my wickedness. My sins might have been considered little things, but they bothered me. Mother would ask me to run an errand and I would say, "Yes, I will do it," and then I'd put it off and not get it done. I also took little items that belonged to my brother, which he did not miss. I felt guilty, and so I wanted to live one day without doing any wrong. To me, this would be living a perfect day. I didn't speak to my parents about my plan, for I felt that it was between my Heavenly Father and me, so I prayed earnestly about it.

It took me about a week to live what I thought would be a perfect day, doing no wrong. As I knelt to say my prayers each night that week, I had to say first that I was sorry but I didn't make it, as each day I had done some naughty things. But as I prayed, I felt a growing sense of emptiness. And on the day that I achieved my goal of not doing any wrong, I felt so unhappy as I knelt to pray that I cried out to my Father in heaven, "Why do I feel so empty and terrible? I haven't done anything wrong. Why am I not happy?"

He answered me in the voice of the Spirit, asking me with perfect gentleness, "What good have you done today?" I thought and thought, and then I cried because I realized I hadn't done one single good thing that day. In my effort to do no wrong, I had done nothing but sit in a corner all day. Through a flood of tears I promised, "Never again will I kneel before you so empty. I will try each day to do good things."

This experience has been a guide to me all my life. I have not always been successful, but I have tried, and I have been grateful to a loving Father in heaven who answered a child's prayer with a question that was to teach and bless for a lifetime.

We do have the power given us to do good. *The power is in us.* We are free agents, and it is our duty and responsibility to do all we can for righteousness' sake and to teach this to our children.

Edmund Burke said, "The only thing necessary for the triumph of evil is for good men to do nothing." We should teach our children this great truth. Each individual must find that area wherein he can do the most good and use his talents to the utmost for the benefit of everyone around him.

Chapter 7

Cultivate Honesty

I have commanded you to bring up
your children in light and truth.
(D&C 93:40)

The Lord has given much admonition and counsel regarding honesty. Lying, being deceitful, bearing false witness, repeating unfounded rumors, and stealing are all condemned. He has said, "Ye shall not steal, neither deal falsely, neither lie one to another. . . . Thou shalt not defraud thy neighbor, neither rob him. . . . Thou shalt not go up and down as a talebearer among thy people." (Leviticus 19:11, 13, 16.)

The Lord's instruction regarding honesty outlines the effect dishonest behavior will have upon us and others. He says: "Thou shalt not steal; and he that stealeth and will not repent shall be cast out. Thou shalt not lie; he that lieth and will not repent shall be cast out." (D&C 42:20-21.) "And if a man or woman shall rob [or steal or lie] he or she shall be delivered up unto the law of the land." (D&C 42:84-86.) Being subject to the laws of the land whether those laws are harsh or lax is the outward result of dishonest behavior.

The dishonest person causes social problems in the community where he lives, but there are personal hurts when deceit and lying occur. In Proverbs 18:8 we read, "The words of a talebearer are as wounds, and they go down into the innermost parts of the belly." Personal reputation can be damaged and conflict and contention arises when lying rumors are propagated. The Lord wants all such things to end. He has said: "Let the lying lips be put to silence." (Psalm 31:18.) "Keep thy tongue from evil, and thy lips from speaking guile." (Psalm 34:13.) "Ye should do that which is honest." (2 Corinthians 13:7.)

Trying to teach our children to do that which is honest can sometimes be frustrating. Suppose that as a mother and her child finish shopping, she discovers in his pocket some candy he took from the grocery store. When she confronts him, he says the grocery man gave it to him, but she knows this isn't true. She wonders, "Where have I failed? Is my child a little thief?"

Instead of assessing blame, she should ask herself: "Why did he take something that was not his? Why did he lie about it? What can I do to make this a learning experience?" It is important to understand that such behavior is not really unusual. To guide a child through such problems, the parent should first try to understand why he acts as he does and then take appropriate corrective measures.

It is not unusual for children to take things that do not belong to them, or to lie to avoid difficult situations. But a school-age child seldom takes a particular object just because he wants it, nor does he lie simply to save face. Usually there is a deeper reason. Children need the help of adults in acquiring the value of honesty. Parents should never be indifferent to or ignore dishonest behavior, thinking the child will outgrow it without help or that he is just going through a stage. They should look at the situation from the child's viewpoint to gain insight as to why he behaved as he did.

A variety of factors are involved in the reasons behind children's dishonesty, including the following:

1. *Envy.* Susie is envious of Sally's new doll, and she wants one too. When she sees one in the store, she tucks it under her sweater and takes it home. Vivian sees others in her group admire Jane's new dress, so she says she has several at home, but her mother won't let her wear them.

2. *Acceptance by friends.* Johnny feels that unless he has a lot of marbles to trade, Sam won't play with him, so he steals to acquire more marbles.

Some of the boys are talking about how rich Brad is and that his new house has a racquetball court in the basement. Jim brags that money is not that hard to come by and that he could earn a hundred dollars a week if he wanted to.

3. *Spite.* Brian is hurt because Steve pushes him down, so he takes Steve's lunch to get even. He does it with an attitude of "I'll show you." Nancy and Laurie are at lunch with two other girls, and the discussion turns to boyfriends. Nancy has dated Steve a couple of times, and now she sees Janet with him. She comments that Janet "will do anything" to get the guy she wants.

4. *No other way.* Darrin sees many interesting and exciting toys and has a strong desire to have them, just as his parents see things they wish to acquire. But Daddy is very careful with money. Darrin thinks Daddy won't give him any money, so he steals because he wants something and feels he can't get it any other way.

5. *Fear of punishment.* Wayne knows he will be punished for coming home late, so he tells his mother that the teacher asked him to stay after school to help with the program the class is presenting next week.

6. *To protect self-image.* Lester, when asked if he took care of his brother as he was supposed to, replies, "Yes, of course." Mother finds out later from Lester's sister, Beth, that Lester went off with friends and left Beth with the responsibility.

7. *Age or stage.* Matt takes a little car home from school because he wants to continue playing with it. "It's mine at

school," he reasons, "so why can't it be mine at home?" When the children at nursery school are admiring the puppies Eric brought for sharing time, David reports that his cat has ten kittens at home, and he describes each one. When the children ask excitedly for him to bring them, he quickly adds, "Oh, they all died."

These are a few of the more common reasons why children resort to lying and stealing. Parents should try to determine the cause for the child's behavior if they desire to guide him toward more positive action. The principles that follow suggest a variety of options in dealing with dishonest behavior and in teaching honesty so that problems do not become more serious.

Principles for Teaching Honesty

1. *Set a clear example.*

Children are more likely to become honest adults if their parents live honestly and set a clear example of being honest.

The people of Ammon were an unusual group of Lamanites who were converted to the Lord. They became totally steadfast and unwavering in their commitment to live the gospel. "They were perfectly honest and upright in all things; and they were firm in the faith of Christ, even unto the end." (Alma 27:22.) From those parents came two thousand young men who joined Helaman as stripling warriors. He called them his sons and told how exceptional they were because "they had been taught by their mothers." (Alma 56:46-48.) Because the parents were devoted to both fully living the teachings of Christ and teaching the principles to their children, the children became as steadfast as the parents. As a people, they were distinguished for their righteousness.

We will have greater success with our children if we are totally committed to living a standard of complete honesty and to teaching it to them. When a child sees that his parents are honest in most things but not all, it is difficult for him to accept the principle of total honesty. Parents who try to teach their children to be honest but who do not themselves live honestly are more likely to have children who, seeing the hypocrisy, will become disillusioned, resentful, and disrespectful toward parents.

2. *Nurture growth and understanding.*

Since some dishonest behavior is a result of a child's age and lack of understanding, parents need to recognize that growth and teaching are necessary to establish standards of honesty. Each child proceeds through specific steps in his growth. During his earliest years, he simply clutches whatever he can grasp as a part of natural curiosity. His first learning experience is through feeling and holding the things around him. By the time he is two or three, parents usually manage to teach him not to touch dangerous objects, but he has not yet learned the clear distinction between "mine" and "thine." In learning property rights, children first need to learn possession. In doing so, they become exasperatingly "mine"-oriented. Once the child learns the word *mine* and the feeling of possession, he says "mine" as he grabs at everything—even the neighbor's toys. When he learns that he can possess, he goes to extremes in wanting everything to be his. (Children begin to take things at this stage simply because they like them.)

As the child enters school, he continues in his desire to have things. Stealing may become a common occurrence with the school-age child. Parents should not be dismayed at such behavior; rather they should view such experiences as opportunities to teach the child honesty. More than one situation will usually occur before the child learns to be honest. With love, support, and continual teaching by precept and example, he can learn to respect others' belongings.

There is also a sequence of learning in telling the truth. The three- to four-year-old develops a vivid imagination. He tends to mix fact and fantasy because he truly cannot tell the difference. His imagination is so vivid that his dreams and fantasies become real. When a child exaggerates, parents should not scold him, because he is not doing so to be naughty. It is simply a result of a growth stage.

Parents can help their child to distinguish between truth and imagination during this period by saying, when he tells a tall tale, "My, that was a fun story! Now I'll tell you something I really did this morning."

Most children exaggerate the truth (or come up with something that has no truth at all) and take things that are not theirs. Whenever dishonesty occurs, parents can use them as prime teaching moments. They should avoid using negative labels, such as liar or thief. As parents give positive encouragement and guidance, children eventually mature and become firm in their commitment to honesty.

3. *Make honesty advantageous.*

Whenever dishonesty occurs, parents should not let it work out to their child's advantage. King Benjamin counseled, "Consider on the blessed and happy state of those that keep the commandments of God. For behold, they are blessed in all things, both temporal and spiritual." (Mosiah 2:41.) The Lord's admonitions to us to be honest are found throughout the scriptures and should help us as parents to nurture this virtue in our children. Proverbs tells us, "They that deal truly are his delight." (Proverbs 12:22.)

We should strive to instill in our children a desire to feel the approbation of the Lord for righteousness. When children can feel the inner glow that comes when they have been honest in the face of temptation, then they will want to continue to be honest. We as parents need to be alert and make certain that our children do not find dishonesty satisfying, even though it is often portrayed in the media as desirable. When a child steals or lies, even in small things, he should feel embarrassed and chagrined at his mistake. If we renounce "the hidden things of dishonesty" (2 Corinthians 4:2), then our children will learn that dishonest behavior does not lead to success or pleasure, but rather to eventual unhappiness.

When children take small things that do not belong to them, or tell little white lies about what they have done, some parents just overlook the incidents. But this attitude is not a kindness to the child. The earlier children get help in dealing with dishonesty, the better. They need to learn the consequences of their deeds. If they continue taking what is not theirs or lying to protect themselves, they may become adept at meeting their needs in those ways, establishing patterns of behavior that could become difficult to change.

Blake had not felt accepted by his peers, so in order to make himself feel and look more important to others, he began to exaggerate the truth. He continued this pattern into his teens. Whenever he did not do as he was asked or got into trouble, he lied about it. This behavior reached a climax one night when his parents were away for the evening and had asked Blake to pick up his sister, Susie, at the bus station as she returned from a school trip.

The next day his mother asked Blake if he had picked up Susie and if everything had gone all right. He said, "Yes, things went fine."

Later his mother learned from a neighbor and then from Susie (who didn't want to tell on her brother) that Blake had, in fact, failed to show up. He had gone out that night with friends, leaving his younger brother home alone and forgetting about his sister. Susie had called the neighbor to come get her.

The seriousness of the incident, added to the many earlier lies about other things, led Blake's father to approach the boy in a personal interview to convince his son of the serious consequences of such behavior. His father's loving concern so touched Blake that through many tears he was able to confess his weakness. As he tried to be more honest, Blake felt better about himself and found he had less need to exaggerate or evade the truth.

When children lie or steal, they should be dealt with in such a way that it is not a pleasant experience. On the other hand, correcting dishonesty should be a good experience, and children should feel confidence in themselves and their ability to live standards of honesty. They should feel that honesty really is the best policy.

4. *Teach property rights.*

Parents can teach their children respect for the property of others both by precept and by example. Paul gives excellent counsel on this: "Let him that stole steal no more: but rather let him labour, working with his hands the thing which is good, that he may have to give to him that needeth." (Ephesians 4:28.) Paul tells us not only what *not* to do (do not steal), but also what we *should* do (work to acquire enough to give to others). These two extremes of stealing and giving to others are related to how we view property.

Respect for the property of others is a basic law in most societies. The law given to Moses is still important for our civilization today. Children must be taught to respect property rights, just as they are taught to conform to other codes of conduct in our society.

In the process of training children to discern what is and what is not theirs, positive experiences are needed to help them develop a sense of possession and then a desire to share what they have. They should feel that some items truly belong to them. Certain toys should be theirs, and they should each have a place of their own in which to keep them.

Within the family, children learn to respect each others' property when their own possessions are respected. If someone takes a child's things without his consent, he may feel justified in doing the same to others.

In teaching a child to share, parents shouldn't be too forceful in making him give toys to another child before he is ready to do so.

Three-year-old Mike screamed, "Jimmy took my new truck. I want it! I want it!" His mother wisely distracted Jimmy, by rolling a ball to him and saying, "Can you catch it? Good! Can you roll it back to me?" Having distracted Jimmy, she then returned the truck to Mike and told Jimmy, "This is Mike's new truck. He wants to play with it now. Perhaps when you visit another day he will let you play with it." She knew that until Mike was ready to share, it was best to provide something else for the other child. Children usually share willingly *after* they feel real possession.

Becky had a difficult time sharing a new doll at school. To help her with this, the teacher gave Becky the doll when she first arrived and announced to the group, "Today the doll is Becky's. She can play with it all day if she wishes. She may share it if she wants to, but she doesn't have to. It's hers alone." As she handed the doll to Becky, she said again, "It's all yours. You don't have to share it, but you can if you want to." The teacher reminded the children several times that the doll was Becky's to share only if she wished to. Before the morning was over, Becky was happily sharing the doll with the other children and with no prompting. Now it was hers to give, and she enjoyed doing so.

As a child learns to value possessions that are truly his own, parents have a sound basis for teaching respect for the belongings of others. When Matt, age five, takes a car from school, the parent might say, "The car belongs to the school just as your bike belongs to you. The car needs to be returned. If someone took your bike, wouldn't you want him to return it to you?"

Sometimes children become so possessive of their own things that they do not move on to the higher Christian attitude of sharing. But feelings of possession can contribute to building attitudes of genuine generosity and willingness to share. The Lord has said, "Thou shalt not covet thine own property." (D&C 19:26.) Parents should try to teach their children to share willingly and gladly.

As suggested in the scripture quoted at the first of this principle (Ephesians 4:28), not only must our children learn not to steal, but they should also be taught to labor so that they can give. This is basic to Christian living. Our attitudes and actions should make it clear that sharing and giving willingly will lead to greater happiness.

5. *Require restitution.*

In order for children to learn to be completely honest, they must be taught to accept responsibility for their wrongdoings and to make restitution. The scriptures teach clearly about the importance of restitution in repentance. The Lord, speaking to the early Saints who were so fiercely persecuted in Kirtland, Ohio, said that their enemies' sins would not be blotted out until the enemies had repented and rewarded the Saints "fourfold in all things wherewith" they had trespassed against them. (D&C 98:44.)

Most children go through some aspects of being dishonest. If we do not teach them to make restitution for their dishonesty, then they may not be fully repentant—and it may therefore be difficult for them to be fully honest later.

Kind assistance and firm direction toward making restitution are vital when incidents of dishonesty occur. Parents should be certain that their child knows he will not be excused from such behavior, and that saying "I'm sorry" is not enough. Restitution must be made if at all possible. Restitution is usually possible in some way when theft is involved, but it may not always be possible with lying.

Our firm attitude of kind concern but strong disapproval should let our child know that his dishonesty is

seriously wrong. We should approach him with a concerned, not a condemning attitude. If we're sure our
child is guilty of a theft, we shouldn't ask, "Did you take
the money from the kitchen shelf?" Such a question may
cause him to further his dishonesty by lying. Instead, we
might say, "The money you took from the kitchen shelf is
not yours. It must be returned. If you need money, ask
me, and we will talk about it."

If we discover that our child has taken something
from a store, we should state calmly and firmly, "The
candy (or other item) belongs to the store. We will have to
take it back." Then we should go with him to the store
and have him return the candy with an apology. This will
likely be a very painful and tearful experience for the
child. Immediately after he has returned the item, we
should tell him it takes great strength and courage to do
what he has just done, and we're glad he was able to do it.

Another alternative in making restitution is for the
child to pay for what he took. Perhaps the candy is half
eaten and is not returnable, or the child is so chagrined,
anxious, and guilty over his misbehavior that paying for
the item would be a better course of action. If his allowance is not sufficient, we should try to provide appropriate and reasonable ways he can earn enough money to
pay for what he has taken as well as enough extra for
some of his wants. (If the child has to use his entire allowance in paying back the debt, he may be driven to stealing
again.)

It is more difficult to accept the responsibility and to
make restitution for lying than it is to deal with stealing.
Lying words cannot be unsaid, and it is hard to rebuild
the trust lost in a relationship through lies.

Most of us have heard the analogy that taking back
lies is like gathering feathers dropped in the wind. A lie is
often not as detectable as a theft and is usually more
difficult to stop. Children must be taught to be sincere in
what they say and in keeping promises. When incidents

of lying occur, we should try to understand why they happened. If he is lying to protect his image, more pressure will complicate the problem. He needs to feel secure enough to risk our disapproval when we learn the truth about what he has done.

To admit to having told a lie takes courage and a sincere desire to do what is right. It takes some children months, even years, to reach that point.

6. *Foster a close relationship.*

Having a close, loving relationship with our children will eliminate many problems with dishonesty. When they feel close to us and we are intimately involved in their lives, there is less need or opportunity for dishonest behavior.

We should be alert to help our children when small incidents occur and not let them develop further. If our relationship is close, we will more easily recognize such problems while they are still small. When a child gets involved in dishonest acts by himself or with others, what he needs most is loving support from his parents.

A mother came to my office in tears over her ten-year-old daughter's stealing. Lynda had gone around the neighborhood asking for donations for a project at school and had collected fifteen dollars. She then went to the store and spent all of it on candy for herself and her friends. Her mother was mortified at Lynda's behavior. With tears streaming down her face, she said, "She has taken little things around the house before, but this was really stealing." She went on to explain, "The divorce was harder on her than the others. She withdrew and brooded after it was final. Her father was violent and frightened her, yet she had an attachment to him. Since I remarried about eight months ago, she has become very difficult. My husband is always kind and gentle to her and lets me handle all the discipline. Lately she has been threatening to leave and go live with her father, and frankly, I'm about to let her."

I asked, "Does she really want to live with her father?"

"No, I know that she doesn't, but it really bothers me when she throws that up at me when I have to discipline her. I'm at my wit's end to know what to do."

I said, "Maybe what she is saying through her behavior is, 'If I am as bad as I can be, will you still want me? Will you still love me and keep me with you?' Perhaps what she needs more than anything is to have you say, 'You're my little girl. I love you, and no matter what kind of problems you get into, I will still love you and want you. I will never send you away to live with someone else.'"

At this, the mother's tears really flowed. I continued, "If you really feel that kind of love for her, then she needs to hear it. I feel confident that if you go home and say these things to Lynda and follow through with loving support to solve this situation, the discipline problem will gradually disappear." She nodded, gave me a grateful smile, and left.

Once we have dealt with the dishonesty, our child should come away from the situation feeling closer to us. Above all, he shouldn't feel he has lost our confidence and trust. We should reassure him that we are there to assist him in any way necessary through the crisis. He should never feel he has to deal with the problem alone. We can express confidence in his ability to correct the mistake. If he has taken candy from a store, for example, we can say, "I can see you feel sorry about taking the candy. I'm sure you can correct the mistake, and I will help you." When he returns the item, he may be so tearful that it is all he can do to hold out the article. We can help by telling the store manager, "He took this without paying for it and he's now returning it. We are sorry this happened."

Perhaps our teenager is not living as we want him to. As Latter-day Saint parents, many of us find it hard to handle our young people's temporary disregard of

Church standards. They feel keenly our disapproval and pressure to live better, and they may lie to protect themselves. This was the case with Keri.

At age sixteen, Keri was caught up in the whirl of dating. She began dating Tony, who liked to go drinking with his buddies and was inactive in the Church. Keri liked Tony very much and was flattered by the gifts and flowers he gave her and the enjoyable activities he took her to.

Keri's father, watching the romance grow much too intense, insisted that Keri accept dates with other boys. She did so half-heartedly. When her father learned more details about Tony and the kind of life he was living, he asked Keri not to date him at all anymore. He explained why and insisted that she stop seeing him. Such an ultimatum pushed Keri to be dishonest with her father.

Tony was out of high school, but he began meeting Keri at school; and when Keri said she was with girl friends, Tony was there too. This finally came to a head when her mother learned by accident that Keri had been with Tony one day instead of with friends as she had said she would be. Tony had dropped her off a few blocks from home so he wouldn't be seen. Her parents discussed the problem and decided they should talk with Keri about the situation. At supper that night her father asked. "What did you do today?"

Keri replied, "I went to the lake with my friends and just did a little sunbathing."

"How did you get home? Melinda was home by noon. I thought you went together."

"I met Julie there and decided to stay a little longer with her. She dropped me off at the corner."

Keri's parents had hoped she would be honest with them, but when she lied, they asked to talk to her privately after supper. Her father started by saying, "Keri, I know that you have been with Tony all day, and that he met you at the lake, and that you left there with him. He is not the kind of fellow you should be dating. He doesn't keep the standards, and he could lead you to real problems."

Keri, defiant and rebellious, replied, "He always treats me with respect, and he never drinks when we're together."

Her mother, sensing Keri's attitude of rebellion, said, "Keri, do you realize what happens inside a person when he doesn't keep his own standards? When you look in the mirror, are you happy with yourself? Is this really the way you want to live?"

At this Keri began to soften, and she burst into tears as her mother continued, "The kind of things you are doing will not make you happy, Keri. Together we must decide on a better way to work things out."

Keri sobbed and sobbed and could talk no more. She went to bed crying. Her father and mother each in turn sat at her bedside giving loving pats and soothing words, reassuring her of their love and concern.

During the following week Keri asked her father if Tony could come and talk with him. As the four—mother, father, Keri, and Tony—sat together, Tony broke the silence by saying, "I want to know if there isn't some way you will let me date Keri."

Her father responded, "Well, Tony, I want Keri to keep the best possible company and to date boys who are active in the Church and keep the standards."

Tony said, "I don't blame you. If she was my daughter, I'd probably want the same thing. But I feel as if you think I'm Satan himself. I always treat Keri with respect, and I haven't done anything with her that was wrong."

Her father said, "Well, if you will go to your bishop and tell him all you need to, and if you will work with him on setting up a plan to put your life in order—attending all your meetings, paying tithing, and doing all you should—then in three months, if you have stayed with your plan, I will let you come over on Sunday night and visit Keri here."

Tony's mouth dropped as he exclaimed, "Three months!"

Keri quickly added, "That's too long!"

Keri's father finally agreed to a month. Tony carried through by seeing his bishop and straightening out his life, and then he and Keri dated until he left for a mission.

As she matured and felt more secure in her own desires to live the gospel, Keri no longer felt a need to be dishonest, because she had nothing to be dishonest about. Her testimony grew as her commitment to the gospel grew. She drew closer to her parents and was able to pass safely through those difficult teenage years when so many leave the Church and become lost in the world. Her parents maintained close communication with Keri during that difficult time, not condoning or ignoring her behavior, but loving and guiding until she felt secure in living the right way.

Our children need parents who are understanding and who will help them uphold the standards of honesty. They need parents who do not condemn or condone, but who will guide through example, love, and kindness.

Chapter 8

Foster Good Sibling Relationships

And ye will not suffer your children
that they go hungry, or naked;
neither will ye suffer that they transgress
the laws of God, and fight
and quarrel one with another.
(Mosiah 4:14)

The relationships our children have with each other are a major factor in the atmosphere of the home. The way they learn to relate to each other in the family is the foundation of their behavior with other people.

The scriptures provide several examples of brotherly relationships and demonstrate what to do and what not to do to develop good feelings between children. The example of Cain and Abel (Genesis 4) shows how jealousy between children can lead to great evil. Laman and Lemuel also fell under the influence of the evil one by their jealousy. Nephi lamented, "Yea, they did murmur against me, saying: Our younger brother thinks to rule over us; and we have had much trial because of him; wherefore, now let us slay him, that we may not be afflicted more because of his words. For behold, we will not have him to be our ruler; for it belongs unto us, who are the elder brethren, to rule over this people." (2 Nephi 5:3.) Laman and Lemuel's prideful desires caused them to be jealous of Nephi, and that jealousy led them away from the gospel.

As parents, we need to be alert to signs of jealousy between our children and take action to alleviate those feelings and foster affection in their place.

Jim bounces into the house and makes his proud announcement to all within earshot, "I made the basketball team!" Mom expresses pleasure in his achievement and comments on the long, hard hours of practice that made it possible. The younger children eagerly ask when they can see him play. But Sam, Jim's older brother, says in a jealous tone, "Yeah, you always were all brawn and no brain."

Susan and Dan come home with a new infant son. After two girls, Dan is very happy to have a boy. But Nan, once the youngest at two-and-a-half years, cries and asks to be held each time Susan picks up the baby.

Although similar occurrences are common in families, as parents we can do much to minimize jealous feelings if we will ask ourselves, What is jealousy and how is it expressed? What causes jealousy? How can I help diminish it and foster affection in its place?

Jealousy is an emotion that most of us feel at some time in our lives. It is complex because it contains elements of anger, fear, and resentment. Jealousy always involves people and is centered in the fear of losing someone's affection or recognition. Jealousy also gnaws at the roots of self-esteem; a jealous child often doubts his own worthiness to be loved.

The face of jealousy has many disguises. Some children express their jealousy very directly. When Mother brings home the new baby, the child says, "Take it back! Can't we get a doggie instead?" He may even try to injure the baby. Other children disguise their jealous feelings in misbehavior. A young child may begin acting like a baby himself: He cries more frequently, demands to be fed, or wets the bed. An older preschool child may conceal his hostility by appearing to be very fond of the new baby, or he may cling to his parents and insist on constant attention.

As children grow older, they may express their rivalry in criticizing, bossing, bickering, or fighting. Stealing and destructiveness may result from jealousy. School-age children may express their jealousy not only at home but also in school. They may feel compelled to get the highest grades, make athletic teams, or get elected class president. Along with one child's excessive desire for popularity, we see opposite extremes of shyness, daydreaming, or withdrawal in another.

Although jealousy has many sources, it often stems from wanting the exclusive love of someone dear. Or it may be caused by just wanting to be equally recognized. Parents sometimes unintentionally show preference for one child over another by attending all the performances of one child; because Dad enjoys basketball, he attends all of Todd's games, but neglects Stan's piano recitals. Nothing makes a child feel less kindly toward a brother than to note that his brother's appearance, manner, and abilities are preferred by his parents. Partiality shown by parents is one of the greatest sources of rivalry among children.

An excellent biblical example is found in Genesis 37:3-4, which reads, "Now Israel loved Joseph more than all his children, because he was the son of his old age; and he made him a coat of many colours. And when his brethren saw that their father loved him more than all his brethren, they hated him, and could not speak peaceably unto him."

It is natural for parents to develop closeness to one child over another because of personality differences, but parents who, because of personality or other differences, show partiality among their children are sowing seeds that may sprout into great envy and bring sorrow and dissension in the family.

Differences in sex, physical and intellectual abilities,

health, appearance, or material possessions can all be
fertile soil for jealousy. We read in Genesis 25:27-28,
"The boys grew: and Esau was a cunning hunter, a man
of the field; and Jacob was a plain man, dwelling in tents.
And Isaac loved Esau, because he did eat of his venison:
but Rebekah loved Jacob." Here again is an example of
parents giving preferential love to children because of
their differences. But from the same differences, affection and cooperation among children can flourish. What,
then, is the secret? How can jealousy be diminished?

Parents are the keys to harmony in the home. Their
attitudes toward their neighbor's new boat or a sister-in-
law's beautiful voice or a friend's lovely hair will be reflected in their children. If Dad is jealous of a neighbor's
boat, Scott may be jealous of Doug's new bike. Parental
attitudes and actions can be decisive factors in promoting
or preventing jealousy within the family.

Principles for Fostering Affection among Children

1. *Help the older children accept the new baby.*

By properly preparing their older children, parents
can do much to alleviate the children's feelings of
jealousy when the new baby arrives. A child can be told
simply, "We are going to have a new baby in our family."
How far in advance he is to be told will depend on his age.
The children will usually enjoy helping prepare for the
new baby, if the preparations are not overdone. Shopping for the baby can be fun, especially if mother picks
up a small item for each of the other children.

When mother and baby come home from the hospital, the father can carry the baby, leaving the mother's
arms free to hug the children, who have anxiously
awaited her return. Emphasis should be put on the older
children's maturity and on the baby's helplessness: "The
baby is very small and can't do anything for himself yet.
We will need to do things for him until he learns. Mother
would be happy to have you children help."

Occasionally parents make the mistake of being

overly protective and possessive with a new baby. By always insisting on holding him themselves, they don't
allow older children to express their natural affection for
the child. Even a two-year-old can hold a new baby for a
minute with help. Helping others usually stimulates love.

If jealousy arises in spite of all the parents' careful
planning, they shouldn't be surprised or disappointed;
instead they should try to reassure the other child of his
place in their affections. As we learn from the scriptures,
jealousy cannot always be eliminated.

2. *Overcome the "one-and-only" desire.*

To foster positive feelings between brothers and sisters, parents should avoid showing preference for one
over the other. Rather, they should show appreciation
and enjoyment for all their children.

A child's desire to completely possess his parents,
which is not unusual, is founded in jealousy. The mis-
directed goal of being the one and only person in someone's affections is often carried into adulthood as the
person seeks a mate. Complete fidelity between marriage
partners is essential to righteousness, but love can
abound among many in a marriage, as with the families
of King David, Solomon, Joseph Smith, Brigham Young,
and many others.

The desire for exclusive love assumes that love from
any one person is a limited commodity, like pie. One has
only so much to pass around. Children can learn that as
one loves, his or her capacity for loving grows deeper.
They can feel within themselves love growing for others
as a mother explains, "When Rob was younger, you got
upset with him because he messed up your things, but
now that he is older, you enjoy doing things together."
The pesky younger brother finally becomes a compan-
ion.

We parents can assure our children of our love and
help prevent rivalry by giving them undivided attention
during special times together. In essence, our actions say,

"Now, this minute, I am yours alone. You have my total love and concern, and I am thinking of nothing else."

During such times we should listen more intently and respond more fully than usual with facial expression and physical touch, concentrating totally on the child. If we are half listening, the child may decide, "Daddy thinks more of those people at work than he does of me." We need to make ourselves available to each child. After school children often need to talk. Most of the time, they will have to share our attention, but if each child has occasional times alone with us, he will be able to share us more readily and will not be so apt to fall prey to jealous feelings.

3. *Treat each child as an individual.*

Affection will usually develop between brothers and sisters if parents recognize and accept each child in the family for his or her individual qualities and point out the strengths of each one.

In the scriptures, we read about the differences between Jacob and Esau: "And the boys grew: and Esau was a cunning hunter, a man of the field; and Jacob was a plain man, dwelling in tents." Their mother, Rebekah, favored Jacob, but their father, Isaac, favored Esau— and this favoritism led to problems. Joseph Smith and his brother Hyrum were different but were still very close. Joseph Smith, Sr., and Lucy Mack must have conveyed love and respect for each boy and his different position and abilities.

Each child is unique. Children are less apt to be jealous if they feel accepted as they are and if they feel they are recognized for their individual abilities. Not everyone can play basketball, sing, or play the violin. Not every child has a quick wit or a gregarious nature. We can help a child feel accepted by showing him that we value his musical ability just as much as we enjoy his sister's friendliness.

Paul complained to his mother, "I can't draw and

Katy draws so well." "Yes," his mother replied, "but you are our cheerful one. You keep our house full of smiles and sunshine. Some of us are good at drawing and some of us are good at helping others to be cheerful. That makes the world interesting. It's good that we are all different."

If we treat each child as a unique individual who has a gift of God, then he will value himself and respect his own abilities. Sibling rivalry will be less apt to occur if our children feel that they are valued for their individuality and unique contributions in the family.

To further avoid envy among our children, we should avoid praising or criticizing one child excessively in the presence of others. When compliments are given to one, we might add a compliment about the others or say, "Each of my children contributes something different to the family. They certainly keep me learning new and exciting things." If children are secure in parental love, then envy and jealousy can at least be diminished, if not eliminated.

4. *Love each child uniquely.*

Rivalry will be lessened if parents will love each child in the manner in which he needs to be loved. Parents love all their children, but there is no need to pretend to love them all in the same way. Children don't yearn for equal shares of love, but want to be loved according to their individual needs. Parents should be willing to meet each child's needs, and should not feel guilty if they give the spotlight to different children at different times. If a child knows he can count on getting affectionate attention from his parents when he needs it, he will recognize and accept without jealousy the necessary attention given to someone else in the family.

Because Mary was born with cerebral palsy, her mother had to spend a great deal of time teaching her to do the simplest things. Mary's sister Dawn became extremely jealous and felt neglected because she thought it unfair that her mother did not spend the same amount of time with her. Their mother, aware of the problem, promised, "Dawn, today I'm going to spend all my time with you." Dawn was delighted, and they began working together on an art project. Mary, who was in another room, started to cry. Dawn saw that her mother did not seem anxious to leave, but instead kept working on the project. Mary's cries continued. Finally Dawn said, "It's okay, Mother. You can go take care of Mary."

Dawn later recalled, "I was never jealous of Mary after that, because I knew that if I needed that much attention, Mother would give it." Her mother admitted afterward that it was extremely difficult not to leave Dawn and go check on Mary. But her efforts paid off in dividends of unselfishness in Dawn and genuine love between her daughters.

5. *Foster family fun and unity.*

Planning for and having fun together as a family will help build positive relationships and provide happy memories for children. The family home evening program of the Church offers ways to build love and feelings of belonging in the family. Work projects, vacations, and family outings also increase love and harmony among the children.

One family rented an orchard where all the family worked cooperatively to harvest the fruit. While working side by side with her children, the mother helped them express their good feelings by saying, "I thought this was going to be hard, but it's been fun with all of us here."

Another family organized a family orchestra, since each of the nine children played a stringed instrument. Their practices and performances created great unity, patience, and love for one another.

Time together on enjoyable trips builds fond memories to be shared and long remembered. Such happy, sharing experiences create bonds of love and lessen rivalry among children.

6. *Teach mutual helpfulness.*

Teaching children to help each other and to share their talents will usually build feelings of affection and love between them.

Nephi and Lehi were the righteous sons of Helaman. They remembered the teachings of their father and were distinguished in the Book of Mormon as brothers of great diligence who labored together to preach repentance to the wicked Nephites. (See Helaman 5:1-44.) Other brothers in the scriptures, such as the sons of Mosiah, Peter and Andrew, and James and John, Christ's disciples, also were united in their love for the Lord and in their diligence in teaching others. (See Alma 25:17; Mark 1:16,19.)

Working together, whether in teaching the gospel or weeding the garden, can create bonds of love. As children work together and assist one another, there is less room for envy and rivalry. We can encourage our children to help each other and thereby develop good feelings among them by suggesting, "Your sister is having difficulty with her math. I know you are very good with numbers, and I'm sure you can help her." If we are careful how we ask, the child will have a feeling of helpfulness and will not respond just to please us.

Parents often expect older children to set a good example and help younger ones in many ways. Alma gave the following advice to his son Corianton: "Counsel with your elder brothers in your undertakings; for behold, thou art in thy youth, and ye stand in need to be nourished by your brothers. And give heed to their counsel." (Alma 39:10.) It is right and good to expect children in a family to help one another, for in the family children can learn to "love one another; cease to be covetous; learn to impart one to another." (D&C 88:123.)

As family members utilize each other's skills or trade services, feelings of appreciation grow and rivalry diminishes. Dan, the older son in a family, was involved in a television show and needed to have his presentation material typed. Pete, his younger brother, was learning to type in school. When Dan asked if Pete would type it, Pete replied enthusiastically and proudly, "Of course!" Their mother said it took the boys half the night because the material had to be perfect, but both were pleased when it was finished. Because Pete was able to share in Dan's experience, the brothers' companionship was strengthened.

Children develop real bonds of love when assistance to each other is encouraged and rewarded until it becomes a natural and constant part of family interaction.

7. *Build satisfaction and self-esteem.*

Parents can encourage positive feelings of genuine self-worth to help protect their children from feelings of rivalry and jealousy. The four sons of Mosiah provide an example for us: "And now behold, Ammon, and Aaron, and Omner, and Himni, and their brethren did rejoice exceedingly, for the success which they had had among the Lamanites." (Alma 25:17.) These young men had the love of God in their hearts and felt no need of envy. Aaron, Omner, and Himni were not jealous of Ammon even though they did not have the same success in their missionary efforts as he did.

As a child learns to feel secure and confident in his own abilities, he will not be tempted to give in to feelings of jealousy. The greatest insurance we can give our children against the festering sore of envy is a strong feeling of self-worth and personal achievement. It is salve to the sore for a child to be accepted, to be recognized for his own abilities, and to be secure in being loved.

We parents have an influential role in determining how our children feel about each other. Our attitudes set the emotional climate of our homes, so we should use all the means at our command to foster affection until jealousy is only a fleeting moment in the lives of our children. As family members work together, play together, and help each other, feelings of unity, loyalty, and pride in each other can become central in our family life.

Chapter 9

Help Children Control Anger

He that is slow to anger is better
than the mighty;
and he that ruleth his spirit
than he that taketh a city.
(Proverbs 16:32)

Although most adults experience anger from time to time, children in particular seem to get angry as they encounter frustrating situations, often because of the limitations of their size, age, or inexperience.

Anger is often expressed with power and force, and when unrestrained, it can sabotage an otherwise noble character. Uncontrolled anger can lead to sin. The book of Proverbs states, "An angry man stirreth up strife, and a furious man aboundeth in transgression." (Proverbs 29:22.) Paul asked, "Can ye be angry, and not sin?" (Joseph Smith Translation, Ephesians 4:26.) This question implies that we are truly in dangerous territory when we become angry.

Knowing that the thought precedes the deed, Christ gave preventive counsel: "Ye have heard that it was said by them of old time, Thou shalt not kill; and whosoever shall kill shall be in danger of the judgment: But I say unto you, That whosoever is angry with his brother with-

out a cause shall be in danger of the judgment."
(Matthew 5:21-22.)

These scriptures help us see our goal as parents to diminish and control our own anger and to teach our children to avoid becoming angry and expressing their angry feelings in inappropriate and destructive ways. When anger does arise, we should direct it into constructive channels.

Principles for Controlling Anger

1. *Control anger in ourselves first.*

Parents' good example will do more to teach their children to be slow to anger than any words they could say.

Someone has said that emotions are more caught than taught. We can give many fine lectures and wonderful family home evening lessons on being slow to anger and exercising patience, but if we ourselves are quick-tempered, our children will not hear our words. Because emotional responses are usually learned through observing and mimicking, our lectures are to no avail.

One mother confessed, "Our little Regina was born with a sweet gentleness and a seemingly natural patience. She rarely cried when she got hungry, but just whimpered or gave one little cry, and then lay quietly until she was fed. She was not at all like her older brother, whose hunger needs were abrupt and who would scream loudly unless cared for immediately. Now that Regina is two years old, her patient disposition has all but disappeared. She is becoming a demanding, short-tempered little girl who imitates my own lack of patience and sharp tongue. I wish I could develop more patience, because I know that my quick temper is a negative influence on my children."

The scriptures are not mild in describing anger and the effects of a bad temper. "A man of great wrath shall suffer punishment." (Proverbs 19:19.) "Wrath is cruel, and anger is outrageous." (Proverbs 27:4.) "Cease from anger, and forsake wrath; fret not thyself in any wise to do evil." (Psalm 37:8.) "It is better to dwell in the wilderness, than with a contentious and an angry woman." (Proverbs 21:19.)

Most parents who have difficulty controlling their anger know that this weakness causes hurt feelings, resentment, and other problems in the family. They may also suffer much guilt after their tempers have flared. Many of us feed our tempers and set the stage for angry scenes by the thoughts we entertain. Self-appraisal, conscious effort, constant vigilance, and sincere prayer may be required to overcome a quick temper. Individuals who struggle with their tempers find that planning ahead by cultivating its opposite, patience, can help in conquering this weakness.

2. *Defer action when angry.*

Parents can teach their children that postponing action when they are angry will give them better control. Proverbs tells us, "The discretion of a man deferreth his anger; and it is his glory to pass over a transgression." (Proverbs 19:11.)

When angry feelings arise, we are often inclined to react harshly, but if we wait a few moments, that delay can allow us to gain enough control to act more wisely. Children react similarly. When a child becomes angry at someone or something, he usually wants to hurt that person or do damage to something. Teaching him to defer immediate action will help him gain composure and act more maturely.

Richard L. Evans said, "One of the safest tonics for temper is time. Many centuries ago, Seneca said, 'The best cure for anger is delay.' And the idea of the counting to ten has been traced back at least as far as Thomas Jefferson, who wrote, 'When angry, count ten before you speak; if very angry, an hundred.'" (*Richard L. Evans: The Man and the Message,* p. 301.)

Many parents find that silently counting to ten gives them better control when angry feelings surge. The time involved in the silent count is enough delay to allow reason to return.

There are other ways to defer action when angry. One is to simply tell the child we're too angry to discuss the problem at that moment.

Ryan left the house early and headed for his Scout meeting. He told his parents, "I'm going by Dan's to pick him up. We're going to the meeting together." Ninety minutes later, Ryan's Scoutmaster called and asked for him. His father said he should be at the meeting. The leader said he had never showed up. His father then called Dan's home and asked to talk to Ryan. When Ryan picked up the phone, his father questioned him about the meeting, and he responded that he had already been to the meeting and was just skipping the basketball game afterward. Ryan's father angrily replied, "That sounds like a lie to me. You come home immediately."

When Ryan arrived home, his father, still very angry, told him, "It's wrong for you to avoid your obligations and then to lie about them. That really upsets me. I'm too angry to discuss it now. Go to your room and think about your behavior, and wait there till I come to talk with you."

The father read the paper to calm down; then he and Ryan's mother went for a short walk to discuss their son's action and to decide what to do. When they returned, he went to Ryan's room and was able to talk with him in an attitude of loving concern rather than anger.

Although Ryan thought the meeting wasn't important and he had lied about his attendance, he was repentant, and he learned a good lesson about not deceiving his parents.

Parents are able to act with better judgment if they defer action when they are very angry. Children also will avoid mistakes and regretful scenes if they postpone responding when they feel angry.

3. *Use a soft voice.*

When children become angry, a parent's soft voice and mild manner will help dissipate the anger. The scriptures tell us, "A soft answer turneth away wrath: but grievous words stir up anger." (Proverbs 15:1.)

Angry situations arise in every family. Uncontrolled anger can cause a person to act irrationally by yelling, name calling, insulting, threatening, or being physically violent. Sometimes when parents speak in anger, they attack the character and personality of the child with such statements as, "You stupid idiot, I told you not to touch that," or "You're such a slowpoke; it's going to take you a year to finish that job," or "Why can't you keep your room clean? You're so messy."

Such expressions of anger can have devastating results. A parent's lack of self-control may cause a child to become rebellious or withdrawn. When a person explodes into an angry tirade and hurls insults or physical blows at another, he may experience feelings of shame and guilt afterward. Such feelings of regret can lead to diminished self-respect as well as the loss of the love and respect of those mistreated.

How foreign from the Spirit of the Lord such angry scenes are! Speaking in uncontrolled anger is indeed contrary to the counsel we read in the scripture to give a "soft answer." Speaking softly when a child becomes angry will usually take the edge off his angry feelings and help him gain control.

Jimmy was building a big crane with his Lego set and was now ready to use it in his play. John, hurrying past, accidentally tripped over the crane and broke it in pieces. Jimmy, in tears and anger, jumped up, waved his fist, and yelled, "You broke my crane. I'm going to smash your face!" John replied in a gentle, quiet tone, "I didn't mean to break it. I'm really sorry. I'll help you fix it." Jimmy calmed down as John started to help rebuild the crane.

We can help our children learn to control and express their anger appropriately by helping them identify their feelings. Mother could say in a gentle tone: "You are angry with Tom because he took the truck you were playing with," or "You are angry with Julie because she borrowed your racquet without your permission, and you had planned to use it yourself. Perhaps you should tell her how angry it makes you when she borrows your things without asking."

Teaching a child to describe the behavior that caused his anger will help him to be more reasonable in what he says and to speak with more control. Our own soft answer and gentle manner will do much to help our children to control their angry feelings and express them appropriately.

4. *Teach socially acceptable responses to anger.*

Children will deal with their anger better if they learn that there are both appropriate and inappropriate ways to express angry feelings. In the Old Testament, we read how "Moses' anger waxed hot, and he cast the tables out of his hands, and brake them beneath the mount." (Exodus 32:19.) Moses was expressing righteous anger when he broke the tablets, for as he came down from Mount Sinai, he saw the sins of his people. His action got the people's attention and caused many to cease their riotous behavior and repent.

There are also examples in the scriptures of unrighteous anger that caused people to inflict harm, as when "Saul cast a javelin at [David] to smite him." (1 Samuel 20:33.) Nephi describes what happened when his brothers were angry with him: "Laman and Lemuel did take me and bind me with cords, and they did treat me with much harshness." (1 Nephi 18:11.) These are examples wherein anger resulted in transgression and sin.

It is best if we are slow to anger and have few occurrences of anger in our homes, but when angry feelings do arise, children need to be taught how to express them appropriately. One way has been mentioned in the previous principle: describing what caused the anger and relating without insult or personal attack how we feel. Though they are angry, children can learn to say politely but firmly, "Stop teasing me; that makes me mad," or, "It makes me angry when you keep bumping me like that. Please stop it."

When children become so angry that any words would be spoken too harshly, physical activity may help dissipate the anger. They might try hitting a punching bag, pounding nails, running around the block, or doing some physical work. Older children can play the piano or engage in sports to express their feelings. After such activity, the youngster may have expended enough energy to be calm and able to talk reasonably about why he was angry.

Mark came home from school angry at his teacher. His mother asked, "What did he do to make you so angry?" Mark replied, "He gave us a huge assignment and then talked the rest of the hour so we couldn't get it done, so now I've got all this homework tonight." He continued to complain angrily. Finally his mother said, "Come and shoot a few baskets with me. I've been practicing, and I'll bet I can match you in a game of one on one." After several minutes outside playing basketball, Mark was able to forget his anger and to do the homework.

5. *Help children to avoid becoming angry.*

Parents can teach their children patience and prayer in order to prevent angry responses from becoming habitual. Some children seem more prone to anger than others. One challenge of parenthood is to teach successfully the spirits that come to us with all their varying temperaments. Although we accept anger as a part of our emotional repertoire, we are counseled to be patient, long-suffering, and slow to anger. Children need help to avoid letting anger become a habitual or frequent occurrence.

Temper tantrums in young children are not uncommon. The toddler's strong, self-centered desires—such as wanting to do things for himself and desiring things that he sees—combined with his undeveloped ability and weak controls, lead to frustration and anger. Parents shouldn't become alarmed when their sweet baby becomes a toddler and begins having temper tantrums. Frequent tantrums might be an indication that he is told "no" too much as he struggles toward independence, or perhaps he is faced with too many frustrations. It might even be that he is predisposed to be short tempered.

In order to help the child avoid becoming unduly frustrated, parents need to analyze the problem. They may need to remove complicated toys and difficult tasks. They might also try to be in tune with his need for independence by letting him do as many things as he can for himself. They can state requests in a positive way, and avoid statements that appear to give a choice when none is intended. For instance, they shouldn't say, "Are you boys ready to come in for dinner?" when they mean, "Boys, dinner is ready. It's time to come in now."

Consistent discipline and punishment will also lessen or eliminate children's frustrations. Inconsistent discipline can be very infuriating to a child. When limits are presented, he will challenge them at first, but when they are firm, those limits can give him security. Consistent discipline also means that parents not give in to a child's angry rage. Angry responses are not rewarded by the child's getting his own way.

Four-year-old Billy, the oldest of three children, had learned that when he really screamed and cried his mother would give him what he wanted. His temper tantrums became more frequent and more violent as he reached his fifth birthday. His mother, at her wits' end, talked about the problem with Billy's grandmother, who lived next door. The grandmother said, "Next time Billy has a tantrum, call me and I'll come right over."

Later that day Billy started another tantrum. His grandmother came and said to his mother, "While you go to the store and get me some flour, I'll stay with Billy." Then she sat in the rocking chair and crocheted and whistled while Billy lay on the floor kicking, screaming, and crying. He completely wore himself out, and when he stopped, she took him on her lap and showed him what she was making.

The next time he started a tantrum, his mother said, "I guess I had better call Grandma." Billy stopped, and gradually the tantrums disappeared.

Children as well as adults lose control of their emotions more frequently when they are tired or fatigued. Good nutrition and proper rest will do much to aid anyone in being slow to anger.

An attitude of tolerance and patience will also help an individual avoid becoming angry. When a child encounters situations and people that are irritating and arouse feelings of anger, he can be taught to take a new look, get a different perspective, and see the situation as less annoying.

Wendell, an only child, was pleased with all his new friends at nursery school. But as time passed, he became irritated at the noise they caused. He said to the teacher, "Make them be quiet! It's too noisy in here." His irritation grew to real anger as he complained more and more about the noise.

One day when Wendell became angry at Sam, who wouldn't be quiet, the teacher took Wendell aside and said, "Wendell, when you are home there are no other children to play with, and it is peaceful and quiet. It is nice for you to have a quiet time at home, but there are times when you wish you had someone to play with. Is that right?" He nodded. "Here at nursery school you

have lots of friends to play with, and there are many
things to do. When you and Jim and Brian play with the
trucks, you have a great time and make a lot of noise. But
that is okay, because when there are many children playing, noise is to be expected. So don't let the noise bother
you; just remember that you can have quiet at home.
Next time it gets noisy, say to yourself, 'It's noisy, but it
doesn't bother me.'"

The next day as Wendell was working with a puzzle
and the other children were noisy with the blocks, he said
to the teacher, "It's noisy in here, but it doesn't bother
me."

Children need to be taught to decide ahead of time
that they will not get angry and will not let something irri-
tate them. Such self-discipline will be easier for some
than for others.

Parents can also teach children to pray for help from
Heavenly Father to overcome a temper. They can feel
that Heavenly Father will indeed help them overcome
any weaknesses or problems they might encounter.

We, as parents and teachers, will come closer to our
goal of being slow to anger and helping our children control their tempers if we take strength from the scriptures.
We read, "His anger endureth but a moment" (Psalm
30:5), and "Let not the sun go down upon your wrath"
(Ephesians 4:26). We are entitled to feel angry without
guilt and shame when we stay in control and are slow to
anger. When anger does occur, if we keep it of short duration and express it appropriately, we will be following
the words of the Lord.

Parents who strive to make love the pervasive feeling
of their home will deal with anger more successfully.
Such a loving environment will be in harmony with these
words: "Charity suffereth long, and is kind; charity en-
vieth not; charity vaunteth not itself, is not puffed up,
doth not behave itself unseemly, seeketh not her own, *is
not easily provoked*." (1 Corinthians 13:4-5; italics added.)

Chapter 10

Teach the Sacredness of Sex

See that ye bridle all your passions,
that ye may be filled with love.
(Alma 38:12)

The physical or sexual relationship in marriage is ordained of God, as we are commanded to "multiply and replenish the earth." (D&C 49:15-17; 132:61-63.) As parents bring children into the world, they desire those children to grow up and worthily fill the measure of their creation by bearing children also.

＊Teaching and guiding their children so that they will use the power to give life in a righteous setting is one of the most difficult tasks parents face. Because of their uneasiness in this delicate area, many parents leave the teaching of this most important aspect of life to others. Many parents warn against immorality but do not know how to help their children be moral. ＊

Children today are exposed to immorality through television, music, movies, and magazines. We cannot totally protect them from exposure to these things, so we must see that they have accurate information and healthy, positive, righteous attitudes to shield them from temptations. They will also be less susceptible to temptation if they are involved in creative activities, such as music lessons, family parlor games, sports, good books, woodworking, and sewing. These are only a few possible activities that can replace time wasted on exposure to immoral and degrading influences.

Our primary goal in sex education is to have our children "practise virtue and holiness." (D&C 46:33.) To have a solid base for righteous living, children must have knowledge and an understanding of God's commandments. As they grow, they can be taught to appreciate their bodies and to accept their physical growth as right and good. They should like their sexual identity—enjoy being male or female—and each should be pleased with his or her life as a male or female.

Children need to have accurate and respectful understanding of human reproduction. They should be taught that sex is a divinely given function, and its use is a sacred trust to be reserved for marriage. To achieve these goals with our children, we find good guidelines in the scriptures.

Principles for Teaching about Sex

✻   1. *Cultivate a communicative relationship.*

Open communication between parents and their children is vital in allowing the parents to give needed guidance in sexual matters. They should establish a communicative relationship with each child so that he feels comfortable in asking questions that are of concern to him as he matures. This relationship should also allow the child freedom to express his sexual curiosity so that his parents may direct it properly. If the child should encounter sexual exploration in group play with other children, he should feel comfortable or confident enough to tell his parents about these experiences.

A child between the ages of six and twelve may be exposed to jokes, misconceptions, and "gutter language." The relationship the child has with his parents should allow him to get accurate information from them and to feel comfortable in sharing negative experiences.

As a child experiences the beginnings of sexual maturity, he needs a parent to explain the physical changes in his body and to provide suggestions for dealing with the strong feelings and sensations he encounters. When young people begin dating and later courting, the wisdom and guidance of their parents can see them through this critical and delicate period. Open and confidential communication is essential in helping children overcome the great temptations that accompany being in love and courting before marriage.

One mother shared with her engaged daughter, Marie, her own difficulties before marriage. She confided, "When your Dad and I became engaged, our love for each other made it extremely difficult to refrain from physical intimacy. As we planned our marriage, those special moments alone together led to increasing intimacy until we found ourselves going too far. Our transgression caused us both much heartache, and it took many years of marriage to overcome the problems it caused." She explained that full confession to the bishop had been necessary before they could cast away this burden of sin. Then she added, "Now that you and Tim are engaged, you too will have moments of great temptation. When this occurs, please come and tell me. I am telling you these things only so you may avoid the heartache we experienced. I know that Satan will seek to destroy your very sacred and divine power to create life."

Later, as the marriage date drew near, Marie was able to come to her mother and tell her, "We were necking last night, and we started to feel ourselves getting out of control. Suddenly Tim jumped up and said, 'I'd better go.' I said, 'Yes, you'd better go.'"

Her mother responded, "Marie, that was the Holy Spirit warning Tim to leave, and you responded to the Spirit also in having Tim go instead of asking him to stay.

I'm proud of you. Plan to be with others as much as you can before you are married to eliminate temptation."

Such confidential communication between mother and daughter helped the daughter past those dangerous moments, and she was able to marry in the temple as a virtuous bride worthy of every blessing and happiness.

*   2. *Nurture appreciation and respect for the body.*

Parents should teach their children that their bodies are a gift from God that should be respected and cared for. The Apostle Paul wrote, "Know ye not that ye are the temple of God, and that the Spirit of God dwelleth in you?" (1 Corinthians 3:16.)

Children can be taught from a very young age that their bodies are special and are "temples of God," and that one of the main reasons they came to earth was to get a body. As the preschool child plays with the sacred areas of his body, as almost every child does, a parent can say, "That's a special part of your body and should not be played with. It's a great blessing to have a body, and we want to take care of it properly."

A kindergarten teacher had her group of children seated around her on the rug talking about the parts of the body. She asked them to point to the various parts of the body and asked, "Where is your temple?" Almost everyone pointed to the spot on the side of the head near the eye. However, one little girl stood up indignantly and said, "No, your whole body's your temple."

Sometimes the child will fidget and play with his body because his underclothing is too tight, or perhaps his genital area has not been cleaned properly and itching occurs. Parents or teachers should make sure that the child's clothes fit comfortably and that he is clean and free from irritation. Then they can distract him with something else. Close supervision of children and the introduction of interesting activities will lead them to feel that other things are more fun, and preoccupation with sexual feelings will recede.

Preschool children are curious about the physical differences between girls and boys. Parents can let them see physical differences by bathing their young boys and girls together. This should be a supervised situation in which children can ask questions and know that it's all right to be curious.

My niece, age five, and nephew, age four, were over visiting and playing in the water. They had their swimsuits on and were jumping on an old inner tube. They had a great time, but their legs became black and dirty. When it was time to clean up, I took them inside to the shower. They were very excited, as they didn't have a shower in their home. Trying to scrub two little bodies without getting in the shower myself was quite a job, so I suggested that they wash each other's backs. There were lots of laughs and giggles as I stood in the doorway trying to see that they were getting clean. There were no overtones of naughtiness or anything inappropriate. Their physical differences were accepted as just how things were. The same two children, a year older, would now be embarrassed to bathe together.

Children will be less apt to play games of "doctor" or "Let me look at you and I'll let you look at me" if they have experiences with the family to see in a healthy, happy atmosphere the physical differences between boys and girls.

<u>Family home evening is an excellent time to talk about proper attitudes and behaviors toward sexuality without pointing the finger and making anyone feel unduly guilty.</u>

The greatest challenges in teaching personal acceptance of one's body come with the changes that occur during puberty. As children mature sexually and experience those changes, they often feel insecure and inadequate, self-conscious and embarrassed. If a child matures much sooner or much later than his friends, he or she will need more attention and guidance from parents.

Some children may feel that they are ugly and unattractive, and parents may need to give assurances to help build confidence or self-acceptance. Before children enter puberty, as well as during the sexual changes of puberty, they need to be strengthened in the commitment to always be morally clean. Lessons on morality at this time may have their greatest impact. Children of ten or eleven are mature enough to understand in more depth the scripture that says, "Man is the tabernacle of God, even temples; and whatsoever temple is defiled, God shall destroy that temple." (D&C 93:35.)

When children feel the stirrings of sexual interest, they can be taught to understand what it means to "abstain from fleshly lusts, which war against the soul." (1 Peter 2:11.) They can also learn that "he that looketh upon a woman to lust after her shall deny the faith, and shall not have the Spirit; and if he repents not he shall be cast out." (D&C 42:23.)

As children mature and develop new, powerful creative feelings, it becomes increasingly important to teach the values of morality and proper conduct. (See D&C 42:22-26; Jacob 3:5-7.) These are very strong forces in our lives, and the proper use and control of sexual behavior is clearly indicated by the Lord. There needs to be balance between teaching that these functions are good and beautiful in the proper context of marriage and teaching that they are degrading and sinful in immoral and unlawful situations. We don't want to scare children into obedience or restraint by morbid stories of sexual immorality, but they do need to know the consequences of such behavior.

As children grow, they can be taught to accept themselves and their bodies with respect and gratitude, to see the sexual aspects in proper perspective, and to be happy and satisfied with themselves as they are.

3. *Instill proper sexual identity.*

As parents accept their own roles as male and female,

their example will help instill in their children good sex-role identification.

The scriptures describe the depth of depravity that some people have reached in regard to sexual behavior: "For this cause God gave them up into vile affections: for even their women did change the natural use into that which is against nature: and likewise also the men, leaving the natural use of the woman, burned in their lust one toward another." (Romans 2:26-27.) This type of behavior is directly related to a person's sexual identity. Satisfaction with one's role, male or female, is basic to a healthy and productive life. This aspect of sexuality is learned mainly through parental behavior, but peers can also have an impact. Parents who are happy in their own lives as husband and father or as wife and mother will give their children healthy and proper models for sexual identity.

Preschool boys may play at being mother, and girls may pretend to be daddy going to work. This early role playing does not indicate sex-role identity problems, but is a child's attempt to understand the proper role of the people in his world. More often we see preschool children imitating their own sex role.

As children enter the world of their peers in the schoolroom, they begin to be influenced by them also. We see sexual identity expressed in children ages six to twelve as they become best friends with members of the same sex and develop some antagonism toward the opposite sex. Disdain for children of the opposite sex is an attempt to separate and define sex roles.

As children leave their childhood and enter adolescence, they focus their efforts and concern on being like their friends. To be accepted by peers, adolescents try to look and act like others their own age. Sexual identity now has a new dimension, as the youths learn to interact appropriately with those of the opposite sex. Physical changes cause new tensions and interaction between young people may become awkward as they learn to deal with their feelings.

Parents who present proper role models and have loving and happy relationships with their children can help their children face each of these problems and can be fairly assured that their sons and daughters will grow up normally and achieve fulfillment in proper heterosexual relationships.

✳   4. *Answer questions with skill and honesty.*

Parents should answer their children's questions about sex promptly and honestly, using the proper terms. They should be calm and assured and respond only to what is asked.

In this sensitive area, children need information given in a way that not only conveys correct understanding, but also (and perhaps more importantly) provides the proper values. When children ask questions, it is not so much what we say as how we say it that will influence them. Sex is a very tender and sacred subject, and it should be presented within those bounds. If we are initially hesitant when a child asks a delicate question about sex, we might say, "That's a good question. Let me think about it for a moment. I would like to talk to you." This gives us a moment to collect our thoughts and decide how to answer. It also assures him that it is all right to ask.

Another suggestion is to answer only *what* children ask, to give the simplest answer possible and not read too much into their questions. We shouldn't let our own, more detailed knowledge of the subject lead us to think that children want to know more than they really do. We can phrase our answers in basic and simple terms and then ask, "Does that answer your question?" As we watch their reactions, we will be able to tell if they are satisfied, confused, or still wanting to talk. It is possible to tell children too much, but sex education is an ongoing process, and we will probably answer the same questions again and again as they grow and want more detail and further explanation.

In Doctrine and Covenants 19:22, we read: "For they cannot bear meat now, but milk they must receive." This principle is true in many areas of learning, and especially in sex education. We don't unload the whole story of reproduction when a child asks, "Where do babies come from?" A simple answer, "They lived with Heavenly Father before they came to us," may be sufficient. Again, taking cues from the child, we will know if our answer has been adequate.

As we discuss sex with our children, it is vital to the relationship of trust that we tell the truth. This is an important goal, but it is not always easy. Children can ask very difficult questions, but if they are smart enough to ask the question, they are smart enough to know the truth in the simplest form, or some explanation of our view on the matter. A little thoughtful contemplation is required to answer some questions, but there is usually a way to reply honestly and still not tell too much.

Another important consideration is proper timing. This is very important in sex education. We want to avoid giving too much too soon, but we don't want to wait so long that our children get inaccurate information from others. We should take our cues from them and answer what they ask when they ask.

It's important that we use correct terms in teaching about sex. The real names for the sex organs and elimination functions convey much more respect than anything we can substitute. Accurate terminology in sex education teaches correct concepts. When we say, "A baby grows from a seed in the mommy's tummy," it is easy for a child to get misconceptions. He may think that since he swallowed a watermelon seed, a watermelon is going to grow in his tummy. Knowing correct terms for

organs and their functions will give children confidence
in understanding these matters when they hear them discussed by peers and others.

  ✳   5. *Teach a proper understanding of the reproductive process.*

  Children as young as three years old may ask simple
questions about babies. As they get older they may ask
more complicated questions, such as, "How does the
daddy's cell join with the mother's cell?" Some parents
may want to answer this question by describing the value
connected with it: "Joining the father's cell with the
mother's is a special way that father and mother love each
other. It is a private, sacred, and very special process that
you do not see that Heavenly Father has planned only for
fathers and mothers."

  Many elementary schools are introducing sex education in their curricula. Such programs can be helpful if
they involve parents. Many schools show films about
menstruation to fifth- and sixth-grade girls and their
mothers. Pamphlets are also distributed that describe for
girls the physical changes they soon will experience. During a question-and-answer period, the girls can get clear,
accurate answers; they all receive the same *true* information. Some schools also provide a film and discussion
time for boys about their bodily changes.

  After these presentations, young people may want
more complete information and understanding of sexual intercourse and the anatomy of both sexes. They may
want to know about adult sexual behavior in its broadest
expressions. An understanding of the physiological
changes is only a part of the teaching children need.
They also need to know the range of good sexual experiences open to them. Of course, as Latter-day Saints we
teach our children to reserve full sexual experience until
marriage, but sexual interest and good feelings can come
from holding hands, walking with an arm around a per-

son, or sharing a goodnight kiss. Many parents feel that these are appropriate expressions of affection between young men and women.

Young people need guidance as they become old enough to arouse sexual interest in the opposite sex. Girls need to know in some degree how their appearance and behavior may affect boys' sexual feelings. Boys need to know how to handle their strong urges and their responsibility to suppress and control sexual excitement. Parents should make clear what behavior they deem acceptable and also what is not acceptable. They may say to their adolescents, "Don't pet," but many young people wonder just what petting is, and to what degree even kissing may be too much.

I once heard a fifteen-year-old girl, just beginning to date, ask, "What do I do when he won't stop?" She liked the boy and didn't want to offend him, but she was concerned about his aggressiveness. Such specific situations are of great concern to parents, and the best way to handle them is to discuss them and offer suggestions earlier, before the daughter finds herself in these circumstances. A girl needs to know how to graciously stop a boy's hands from going where they shouldn't. Some girls fear the boys will become angry and not date them again if they stop the boys' pursuit. Some boys fear girls will view them as unmasculine if they are not aggressive.

Young people need to know clearly the consequences of adult sexual behavior. Their new creative urges and abilities are a big responsibility. The Lord has made it clear in the scriptures that sexual sin is the sin next to murder. Bringing life into the world and taking life out of the world have such serious and irreversible consequences that he has given clear direction and firm restrictions regarding these acts. (See Exodus 20:14; Jacob 3:12; D&C 49:15-17; 93:35.) True happiness can be achieved only if these creative forces are properly controlled, directed, and expressed. The scripture that states, "bridle all your passions, that ye may be filled with love" (Alma 38:12), can help teach youth the reasons for proper control. Uncontrolled sexual urges not only destroy love but may also devastate the entire life of an individual.

The commandments regarding sexual behavior are clear, but parents can further assist their young people by translating a commandment into "What do I do right now in this situation?" Young people frequently need this kind of direct talk.

For our children to have proper understanding of the reproductive process, they must have an eternal perspective. Family home evening is a good time to explain more about morality, immorality, perversion, the law of chastity, self-control, true love, and celestial marriage. Although these values are taught every day by word and deed, using the scriptures to teach these truths will help our children understand the magnitude of sexual behavior.

Today it is difficult for families to maintain this right and holy view of love and sex. But if we take direction from the scriptures and other good books written by our prophets and teach our children these vital truths, they will more likely want to live virtuous lives.

Chapter 11
Build a Positive Self-Concept

Remember the worth of souls
is great in the sight of God. (D&C 18:10)

The best foundation for a positive self-concept is a true understanding of who we are. Teaching our children about their divine origin as children of our Father in heaven can give them a greater sense of personal respect and dignity. What a difference it would make if each child were to realize that he once lived in the presence of God, as His loved and adored child, and was worthy to come to earth and receive a body as a sacred blessing and privilege.

We read in the Bible that God is the father of all spirits. Children have concrete knowledge of their earthly fathers and can comprehend a Heavenly Father. Singing "I Am a Child of God" is good instruction for any child as he learns his origin and purpose here on earth.

We learn in the Pearl of Great Price that our spirits were created and lived as organized intelligences before the world was. We are also told that the Lord promised that those who were faithful in that premortal world would be added upon by having physical bodies in this second estate. Furthermore, if they would keep the commandments of God taught by the revelations, they would have "glory added upon their heads for ever and ever." (Abraham 3:26.)

President Harold B. Lee, expounding these truths further said: "You are now born into a family to which you have come, into the nations through which you have come, as a reward for the kind of lives you lived before you came here and at a time in the world's history, as the Apostle Paul taught the men of Athens and as the Lord revealed to Moses, determined by the faithfulness of each of those who lived before this world was created." (*Ensign,* January 1974, p. 5.)

No matter what else we do, if our children do not like themselves, we will fail in our efforts to teach the first and second greatest commandments, to "love the Lord thy God" and "love thy neighbour as thyself." (Matthew 22:37-39.)

Principles for Building a Positive Self-image

1. *Establish positive relationships.*

Parents love their children, but close, warm relationships that build positive feelings of self-worth in a child do not spring automatically out of parental love. Much effort and unselfish time and devotion, along with communications of deep love from parents, are needed to build that all-important relationship.

One couple truly paid the price in love and unselfish time to develop and sustain such a relationship with their teenage daughter, Anna. Many evenings after supper they would sit around the table and eat popcorn or nuts while they discussed the happenings of the day. Then the mother noticed that Anna was becoming somewhat withdrawn and showed signs of tension. One day she said she had been asked to go to a football game with some friends. When her mother asked who the friends were, Anna seemed to be evasive and defensive. Her mother thought it over and said, "No, I don't feel you should go to the game, but please invite your new friends over so Dad and I can meet them and get to know them."

This only seemed to create more tension in Anna. As the days passed, the tension mounted to the point that her mother could stand it no longer. She said to Anna, "What's wrong? Something is bothering you. Please, let's talk about it." Anna, upset and troubled, burst into tears. Her father joined them as she finally confessed, "My new friends at school are after me continually to join with them in their activities. Some of their activities sound really fun and I would like to go, but they put tremendous pressure on me to do things I know are not right."

Her father put his arm around her and asked, "Do you truly want to go with these friends? Are they uplifting and strengthening to you? Do you really want to be involved in what they are doing?"

Through her tears she admitted, "No, Dad, they really are not the kind of friends I want."

"Then," said her father, "you must let them know how you feel—that you don't want to do the things they are doing. They will quit putting pressure on you if you let them know how you feel. Instead of spending your nights chasing boys and going to poor movies, I'd rather you'd develop the talents that you have, such as sewing and playing the piano and being a shining example to others. I love you very much. I love you more than any teenage girl I know. You are beautiful, and I don't want you to do anything that would tarnish your beauty or your character. If ever again peer pressure becomes tough, please come and talk about it with us. Even if you think we won't understand, give us a chance."

In the atmosphere of true love and inspiration, Anna's parents were able to help her strengthen her goals and lift her spirits so that she was able to decline the invitations of her peers and gain their respect. Her confidence in herself became more secure as she developed feelings of true self-respect.

The teenage years are a critical time for parents to stay close to their children. It is important that children are not discouraged or demeaned as they seek answers to questions the parents have long since resolved. Such seeking is a necessary part of growing up. Youths must now put in adult perspective values they accepted earlier without question. They question many things as they try to decide for themselves.

For many young people, adolescence is a painful period, while for others it is a happy time of growth and fun. The adjustments may cause self-consciousness, inferiority, stress, and anxiety. Once young people answer "Who am I?" in a positive way, life becomes more stable and satisfying.

2. *Provide encouragement.*

In Proverbs 16:24 we read: "Pleasant words are as an honeycomb, sweet to the soul, and health to the bones." Encouragement is indeed "health to the bones" to all of us. Growing children need to be encouraged to feel good about themselves. Scriptural examples of encouragement can apply to every aspect of life and provide a sure guide in nurturing our children. Let us not overlook this familiar yet powerful principle in rearing happy children who know their own worth.

3. *Use discipline and punishment wisely.*

Many times the things we do to discipline or punish our children result in damage to their self-esteem. Discipline should be administered in such a way as to redirect negative behavior toward more positive action that will give the child confidence in correcting his mistakes.

Every child acts at times in inappropriate ways and does some downright "bad" things. But when those times occur, we should not punish in such a way as to destroy or damage a sensitive and growing self-image.

Kyle was sitting at the breakfast table when he accidentally bumped a glass with his elbow and knocked it off
the table. It broke with a clatter that startled everyone.
His mother snapped, "Oh, no, not another glass!" Kyle
said, in guilty apology, "Oh! Why do I do such terrible
things? Sometimes I just hate myself."

One criterion in deciding on discipline or punishment
might be to ask ourselves: "How will he feel about himself if I do this? Will he feel better eventually and grow to
like himself more?" If what we do or how we do it makes
the child dislike himself or damages his self-confidence,
we are definitely using the wrong approach. In all of our
interactions with our children, this seems to be the area
in which we can damage their self-concept most severely.
We must become aware of and stay alert to the child's
feelings about himself.

Often we are quick to stop bad behavior but not as
quick to make sure that the child feels good about himself when the behavior is ended. A child will usually feel
sorry about what has happened, but the outcome in the
long run should be better behavior and better feelings
about himself. Because good feelings don't immediately
replace guilt or remorse for wrongdoing, parents tend to
forget about them, so they don't develop at all.

Chad was continually causing problems at school, in
Primary, and at home. He always seemed to be caught
doing the wrong things and to be scolded for them. One
day as he hugged and kissed his one-year-old brother, his
mother overheard him say, "I love you. I love you more
than I love me!"

The Lord said, "Love thy neighbour *as* thyself."
(Matthew 22:39.) To love someone more than we love
our own selves can be hurtful. Chad didn't like himself at
all. After being repeatedly corrected in negative ways, he
had developed vague and painful feelings that told him
he was "no good." His unhappiness might have been
avoided if his parents had been more alert to his feelings

about himself and had counteracted them with experiences and statements that said, "I like you! You can do many good things."

If a child is "reproved with sharpness" and then given "an increase of love" afterward (see D&C 121:43), he will be reassured that his parents do still like him, and he can thereby conclude that he is not a terrible person. He needs to hear from his parents, especially after bad behavior, that they still love him, have confidence in him, and consider him to be a person with great potential and worth.

All of us, even parents, fall short, but we all can repent and still like ourselves. We must teach our children to love themselves, to repent for mistakes, and to grow. Then true self-esteem will be a natural reward.

4. *Encourage proper expression of both negative and positive emotions.*

If a child grows up so inhibited that he cannot express his love for someone, he will also have negative feelings about himself. If he cannot control his temper and becomes angry at his friends for little things, he will probably also be angry at himself. Good emotional control and expression are important to a positive self-image. All of us struggle to keep our emotions in control. Yet we must also avoid being too inhibited to properly express sensitive and tender feelings without shame or fear of ridicule.

Proper emotional expression is a delicate balance, and each child has a particular trait he or she must develop or control. Scott gets frustrated easily if he cannot succeed immediately when making a model, working on homework, or doing any number of things. His mother has tried to help him conquer his frustrations and change his emotions when he feels them swell up inside. They've discussed the problem several times and concluded that when Scott starts getting frustrated and then very angry, he can avoid those feelings by starting to sing.

When he feels himself getting angry, he sings "It's a Holly, Jolly Christmas," because, as he said, "I can't feel mad singing that song." With his feelings under greater control, Scott has gained more self-confidence and self-esteem.

Laurel has a special empathy that draws people to her. Many friends find she is a good listener when they need one; she truly feels concern for them. When she was younger, Laurel sometimes got so involved in others' difficulties that she worried to the point of causing herself health problems. Her mother tried to help her appreciate her special gift. She explained that Laurel might be called upon many times in her life to give comfort and counsel, and that to do so effectively, she should train herself to listen without becoming overly involved. Laurel's special empathy is a trait that needs proper expression and control to be a real blessing in her life. As she matures, she is becoming able to give loving concern without undue worry.

Every mother sees in her children emotions that she can help to direct and to control, so that they grow up with positive and happy emotions.

5. *Stimulate productive activity.*

We can help our children to be involved in productive activity that will give them feelings of competency and contribute to a positive self-image. In the Book of Mormon we read that Nephi caused his people "to be industrious, and to labor with their hands." (2 Nephi 5:17.) Many other groups of righteous people have also been instructed to be industrious and to labor diligently, such as the Israelites, the people of Alma, the Jaredites, and the Latter-day Saints. (See Exodus 20:9; Mosiah 2:18; 23:5; Ether 2:16; D&C 52:39; 64:25.) Brigham Young advocated hard work; he taught that many of the ills of society could be eliminated if people would work hard in a good cause.

Doing something constructive is good insurance

against inferiority. If a child is involved in a worthwhile activity, he will more likely feel good about himself, unless he encounters unfavorable comparison, is belittled, or experiences some other form of unpleasantness. Every child needs to feel that he is good at something.

My husband decided to build a combination storage shed and play hut for our younger boys. He wanted to use the project as a chance to work especially with our eleven-year-old son, to teach and encourage him in carpentry skills and good work habits. In the planning stages, my husband asked our son for his opinions and ideas. As construction began, our son was enthusiastic. All of us, mother and daughter included, worked together on the project, and we as parents found it an excellent opportunity to compliment quickness in understanding instructions, cooperative effort, and steadiness at work.

There were times when our son was careless with tools and had to be reminded to put them where they would be safe and would not injure anyone. The reprimands were given with comments on how well he had worked earlier. His enthusiasm for the project stayed strong, even though he worked many long, hard hours and gave up hours of play and free time with his friends. He felt real pride in accomplishment when the play hut was finished, for the plans had worked out well, the hut looked good, and he knew he had contributed a great part of the work. Because he was praised and complimented often as we worked, he gained confidence in some of the skills his father had tried to teach him.

Constructive activity, such as music lessons, yard work, gardening, or baking, will do much to foster in the child positive feelings of confidence and self-worth.

6. *Teach the "law of compensation."*

The Lord instructed Moroni, "I give unto men weakness that they may be humble; and my grace is sufficient for all men that humble themselves before me; for if they humble themselves before me, and have faith in me, then will I make weak things become strong unto them." (Ether 12:27.) This scripture indicates that our weaknesses are given to us for a purpose—to help us develop humility and faith. The struggle to overcome or compensate for a weakness is often a critical factor in a person's spiritual development.

Moses was keenly aware of his weakness when the Lord asked him to speak to Pharaoh and to lead the children of Israel out of Egypt. Moses responded, "I am not eloquent, . . . but I am slow of speech, and of a slow tongue." The Lord, understanding Moses' weakness, provided for him a spokesman. (Exodus 4:10-16.)

Nephi, on the other hand, was a powerful speaker but was not "mighty in writing, like unto speaking." Still he exercised his faith and said, "The words which I have written in weakness will be made strong unto them [my people]; for it persuadeth them to do good." (2 Nephi 33:1, 4.)

These great leaders were instruments of God in achieving his eternal purposes, and they themselves became spiritually sanctified through their service, notwithstanding their weaknesses.

The examples of Moses and Nephi and others should give us all courage as we struggle with our own weaknesses. And as parents, we can teach our children who are struggling with weakness to press forward with greater fervor, knowing that, with the Lord's help, all things are possible.

All around us are examples of outstanding individuals who have developed strength in one area to compensate for a weakness in another area. Because of Brent's deep feelings of inferiority and insecurity, he did poorly in school. Rejected by his peers, he lived in the world of books. But as he reached his late teens, his struggle to become accepted had matured him, and he became an enthusiastic leader in his stake's youth activities. As an

enthusiastic and willing worker, he finally found acceptance and appreciation for his efforts. He was the one
who gave spark and enthusiasm to whatever activity was
planned.

7. *Teach true repentance.*

An understanding of true repentance is vital if a child
is to build and maintain self-respect. All of us do things
we wish we hadn't, and find that we need to do some repenting. Children who understand the principles of the
gospel will, when they break the commandments, be unhappy with themselves and will carry a burden of guilt
until they fulfill the requirements of repentance.

No one can feel fully good about himself if he is worried about sins he has been or is involved in. A positive
self-concept that has been developed and nurtured
through the growing years can be destroyed if, as the
child grows into independence, sin creeps in. But, as the
scriptures say, "All have sinned, and come short of the
glory of God." (Romans 3:23.) Through repentance, we
may still—if we have not committed the unpardonable
sin—reach the highest goal of eternal life and glory.

We should teach our children the steps of true repentance, as all will have need of repenting to maintain self-
respect. They should be taught that repentance means to
forsake sin (not do it again) and also to confess sin (to tell
the proper person about the sin).

A mother related this experience: "I was driving
along with Jimmy, my eleven-year-old, and we were talking about some pretty important eternal concepts. After
a while he said, 'There is something that has been eating
at me for about a year now that's really bad. I think I
should tell you. Should I tell you now?'

"I said, 'Yes, please do.'

"He told me that he had found some pornographic
magazines one day down by the railroad tracks, and that
he and his friend had looked at them, and then they had
hidden them. I said I was glad he had told me. We then

talked about the evils of pornography and how it was important for him to keep his mind clean and free from unclean and evil pictures.

"I also said that whenever he did something wrong, he should talk to Heavenly Father about it. If it was a serious moral transgression, he should always talk to the bishop. And it is also good to be able to talk to his parents. Talking about transgressions is one step in repentance, I told him.

"He said, 'Yeah, I feel better now; I didn't know I was supposed to tell someone. I'm glad I told you.'

"I went on. 'You know how you felt better, almost lighter, right after you told me?' He nodded. 'Well,' I continued, 'that's why confession is an important part of repenting, because if you carry the burden of sin, you will not feel better until you tell your parents or the bishop, even though you don't do it any more.' He agreed, and we felt closer through the experience."

A complete understanding of repentance needs to include knowing that the Lord truly forgives, and that the individual need not worry about past sins any further except to keep himself from sinning again. Too many have been taught the doctrine that once one has sinned, he can never be whole again. This could not be the doctrine of Christ, because such a doctrine destroys hope and self-respect. "Nevertheless, he that repents and does the commandments of the Lord shall be forgiven." (D&C 1:32.)

Children need reassurance that their sins will be forgiven and that the Lord will remember them no more. (D&C 58:42.) Self-respect will not return if they do not understand and believe this principle.

As a freshman at BYU, Bob heard a talk in stake conference on repentance. The stake president spoke about forgiving ourselves once we have fully repented. He said that thoughts would arise in our minds, telling us, "You're no good! It's no use, you'll never be the same.

Give up—you'll never make it now." He said that these were the doctrines of Satan and that Satan would have us feel worthless and unworthy. We should cast off such feelings and be assured that Christ still loves us, and that we can become worthy through righteous endeavors and keeping the commandments. He admonished the students to say, as did Nephi, "Awake, my soul! No longer droop in sin. Rejoice, O my heart, and give place no more for the enemy of my soul." (2 Nephi 4:28.) This was a real revelation to Bob, and it helped him to gain better self-respect.

Children need to be taught not only to be worthy of forgiveness, but also to be forgiving of themselves. Karl was especially burdened by the sins he had committed before joining the Church. He prayed often and fervently to be forgiven. When he received his patriarchal blessing, he was told that if he would be humble, the Lord would take the memory of his former sins from his mind. This greatly relieved Karl and gave him the strength to overcome his feelings of past guilt.

8. *Foster righteous living.*

Parents should teach their children that living righteously in every way will bring them happiness and, as a natural consequence, genuine feelings of self-worth.

Can you imagine what it would be like to feel confident in the presence of God? Virtuous, righteous living is the key that will give us that confidence. (See D&C 121:45.) We will be assured of our own worth because we have proven ourselves worthy.

As a child, I went with my family to visit some relatives I had never met before. Before we arrived, Mother told us a little about them and said that they were temple workers. That impressed me very much, to think that they worked almost every day in the temple. When we arrived, the man was especially warm and kind. While my parents visited, I sat with my brothers and sister just looking and listening. I couldn't take my eyes off the man. He had a special glow in his face—clear, almost transparent. I concluded, as I thought about what my mother had told me of him, that he was a pure and righteous person. We talked about him on the way home, and my mother assured me that my assessment was correct.

In spite of diligent efforts to teach the gospel to their children, some parents have moments of discouragement or despair when a child makes bad choices and becomes involved in sin. One father experienced deep despair when his son became involved in serious transgressions. The boy's mother said, "Remember the scripture, 'Train up a child in the way he should go: and when he is old, he will not depart from it.'" (Proverbs 22:6.) The father retorted, "But he has departed from all we have taught him." The mother's faith was evident in her response: "But the scripture says, 'when he is *old,* he will not depart from it,' and he's not old yet." A few years later the mother died, but the father lived to see his son come the long way back through repentance into full activity and fellowship in the Church.

In all their great love and faith in rearing their children to be righteous, parents should never give up on a child even when that child has turned against all that he has been taught and seems to be beyond reach. They must exercise patience and endure to the end. It will help if they strive to have an eternal perspective as they see life's events unfold.

I was in college before I read the Bible from cover to cover. As I read, verse after verse sounded familiar to me. I wondered, "Why is this so familiar when I've never read it before?" Then I came to this passage and realized that my parents had followed it: "These words, which I command thee this day, shall be in thine heart: and thou shalt teach them diligently unto thy children, and shalt talk of them when thou sittest in thine house, and when thou walkest by the way, and when thou liest down, and when thou risest up." (Deuteronomy 6:6-7.) The words of the Lord were such a natural part of our family discussions, and I had heard them quoted and expounded so often in Church, that they had become an integral part of my thinking.

As we strive to teach our children to live the gospel and listen to the words of the prophets, we can have moments of great joy in our homes right now. My husband once took our older sons to the Saturday night priesthood session of general conference. Jerry, age nine, and I were left home alone. As we sat on the bed together talking, Jerry asked about what happens at a priesthood meeting. I explained, "President Kimball and some of the twelve apostles will be there and will give special counsel just for fathers and sons who hold the priesthood. It is a special privilege to be able to attend." We discussed other spiritual things, and we both felt a special, sweet spirit. As we ended our talk and walked arm in arm from the room, Jerry said, "This is what heaven's like, huh, Mom!"

Heaven in our homes can happen if we "feast upon the words of Christ" (2 Nephi 32:3) and strive to live so that the Spirit of the Lord can be there. And as we have the Spirit guiding us, our children will feel its influence and will be nourished in their desire to always be worthy and faithful.

May we always strive to follow the Lord's commandment and thus receive his great promise: "Train up a child in the way he should go: and when he is old, he will not depart from it." (Proverbs 22:6.)

Bibliography

The scriptures provide excellent counsel for parents as they "train up" their children. Especially helpful is the topical guide section of the new LDS edition of the King James Version of the Bible (1979). You may wish to refer to the following topics for each chapter in this book.

Chapter 1, *Establish a Loving Relationship:* "Children," pp. 57-58; "Family, Children, Responsibilities toward," pp. 137-38; "Family, Love within," p. 138.

Chapter 2, *Listen and Communicate:* "Communication," p. 69; "Understand," pp. 545-46; "Understanding," pp. 546-47.

Chapter 3, *Give Encouragement,* and chapter 4, *Help Fight Discouragement:* "Cheerfulness," p. 56; "Hope," pp. 217-18; "Trust," p. 539.

Chapter 5, *Provide Discipline and Punishment:* "Chastening," pp. 55-56; "Correction," p. 77; "Justice," p. 274; "Punish, Punishment," pp. 401-2.

Chapter 6, *Instill Responsibility:* "Accountability," pp. 4-5; "Dependability," p. 96; "Duty," pp. 112-13; "Responsibility," p. 424; "Stewardship," p. 500.

Chapter 7, *Cultivate Honesty:* "Deceit, Deceive," p. 91; "Honesty," p. 216; "Integrity," p. 231; "Lying," pp. 301-2; "Stealing," p. 499.

Chapter 8, *Establish Good Sibling Relationships:* "Brethren," pp. 43-44; "Brotherhood and Sisterhood," pp. 45-46; "Family, Love within," p. 138.

Chapter 9, *Help Children Control Anger:* "Anger," p. 11; "God, Indignation of," pp.175-76; "Indignation," p. 226; "Wrath," pp. 592-93.

Chapter 10, *Teach the Sacredness of Sex:* "Adulterer, Adultery," pp. 6-7; "Chastity," p. 56; "Homosexuality," p. 216; "Marriage," p. 309; "Marriage, Fatherhood," pp. 309-10; "Marriage, Motherhood," pp. 310-11; "Sexual Immorality," p. 467.

Chapter 11, *Build a Positive Self-concept:* "Man, a Spirit Child of Heavenly Father," p. 305; "Man, Potential to Become like Heavenly Father," p. 307; "Worth of Souls," p. 591.

Selected Books

Bernhardt, Karl L. *Discipline and Child Guidance.* New York: McGraw-Hill, 1964.

Breckenridge, Marion E., and Murphy, Margaret. *Growth and Development of the Young Child.* Philadelphia: W. D. Saunders, 1963.

Briggs, Dorothy C. *Your Child's Self-esteem.* Garden City, N. Y.: Dolphin Books, 1975.

Children's Views of Themselves. Edited by Monroe D. Cohen. Washington, D. C.: Association for Childhood Education International, 1972.

Dreikurs, Rudolf. *Coping with Children's Misbehavior.* New York: Hawthorne Books, 1972.

Dreikurs, Rudolf, and Soltz, Vicki. *Children: The Challenge.* New York: E. P. Dutton, 1964.

Eyre, Linda, and Eyre, Richard M. *Teaching Children Joy.* Salt Lake City: Deseret Book, 1980.

——————. *Teaching Children Responsibility.* Salt Lake City: Deseret Book, 1982.

Ginott, Haim G. *Between Parent and Child.* New York: Macmillan, 1965.

Gordon, Thomas. *Parent Effectiveness Training: The Tested New Way to Raise Responsible Children.* New York: David McKay Co., 1970.

Griffin, Glen C. *You Were Smaller than a Dot.* Salt Lake City: Deseret Book, 1980.

Griffin, Glen C. and Griffin, Mary Ella. *About You . . . and Other Important People.* Salt Lake City: Deseret Book, 1979.

——————. *Not about Birds.* Salt Lake City: Deseret Book, 1979.

Hymes, James L., Jr. *Teaching the Child under Six.* Columbus, Ohio: Charles E. Merrill, 1974.

Krumboltz, John D., and Krumboltz, Helen. *Changing Children's Behavior.* Englewood Cliffs, N. J.: Prentice-Hall, 1972.

Madsen, Clifford K., and Madsen, Charles H., Jr. *Parents and Children, Love and Discipline: A Positive Approach to Behavior Modification.* Boston: Allyn and Bacon, 1970.

McConkie, Bruce R. *Mormon Doctrine.* Salt Lake City: Bookcraft, 1966.

McKay, David O. *Secrets of a Happy Life.* Compiled by Llewelyn R. McKay. Salt Lake City: Bookcraft, 1967.

Papalia, Diane E., and Olds, Sally W. *A Child's World: Infancy through Adolescence.* New York: McGraw-Hill, 1975.

Pinegar, Ed J. *You, Your Family and the Scriptures.* Salt Lake City: Deseret Book, 1975.

Smith, Joseph Fielding, Jr., and Stewart, John J. *The Life of Joseph Fielding Smith.* Salt Lake City: Deseret Book, 1972.

Young, Brigham. *Discourses of Brigham Young.* Compiled by John A. Widtsoe. Salt Lake City: Deseret Book, 1954.

Viorst, Judith. "What's a Good Mommy?" *Redbook,* October 1974, pp. 38-40.

Webster's New Collegiate Dictionary. 7th ed. Springfield, Mass.: G. & C. Merriam Company, 1973.

Index